Sri Muruga

By

Rahul Kabade

Sri Muruga

Published: 1st Paperback Edition, September 2012

ISBN: 978-0-9573794-0-4

Sri Muruga Publications
150 Wembley Hill Road
Wembley, Middlesex, HA9 8EW
United Kingdom
+44 (0) 77 481 05281
author@srimuruga.com

Rahul Kabade

Dedicated to Satguru Sri Sharavana Baba

of

Sreekrishnapuram, Palakkad, Kerala, India.

www.srimuruga.com

I was introduced to Lord Murugan worship in year 2007. Over the past five years, with the Guru's grace and Lord Murugan's blessing, I have been able to compile this book which answers many of the basic questions any new devotee would have about Lord Murugan. This book is a limited attempt to describe the legend, birth, divine play, popular stories, prominent temples, common festivals and characteristics of the infinite Lord Murugan.

✳

"There is only one religion - the religion of Love. There is only one language - the language of the Heart."

Satguru Sharavana Baba

Preface

In 2007, I met Satguru Sri Sharavana Baba, who is widely believed to be a living incarnation of Lord Murugan of our times. My first meeting with him was extraordinary and memorable. I immediately fell in love with Muruga.

Over the years I had the fortune and grace of the Guru to visit several temples of Murugan in South India and subsequently in London, as well as various countries in Europe. During these pilgrimages and short visits, I was always accompanied by other devotees, most of whom spoke fluent Tamil or Malayalam and very little English. My mother tongue is Marathi and most literature about Muruga was either in Sanskrit, Malayalam or Tamil. So communicating and understanding was a big challenge. Hence, much of my understanding and learning of Lord Muruga, his various names, divine plays, significance of temples, festivals and worship was through thousands of such disparate and loving sources.

During my travel, I was troubled by the scams and corruption that plagued India. However, the best spiritual wealth still survives in this day and age. Spirituality and religion is almost a subject of mockery in media. What I see are symptoms. The root cause is forgetting core values, that which our saints and seers held very dear. These values are in our mythology and scriptures as wisdom and these can bring about a meaningful transformation of the individual from within. A transformed individual will be the seed for transformation of the state. The search for this spiritual wealth and wisdom became my inspiration.

There are very few books in English, even today, that could provide a comprehensive understanding of the glory of Lord Muruga. Some books record the legendary birth of Muruga, while some carry excellent stories from Skanda Purana while some are tourist guides on temples and festivals. I had to read multiple books, research the World Wide Web and consult devotees, priests and experts simply to connect events and figure out the esoteric meaning of various festivals, *mantras* or offerings made during worship of Lord Muruga. I was baffled with Tamil and Sanskrit names and equally baffled on how to approach the worship of Lord Muruga.

One single resource which would provide me a simple and good understanding of Lord Muruga was missing. This inspired me to compile this book. I hope other devotees who are in a similar position as I was in my early days of understanding the divinity of Lord Muruga will find some direction and succor from this effort.

It took me many months to list down the questions I have had through my journey. The answers to those questions have resulted in this book. I hope readers find this humble effort rewarding. While I have taken the utmost care to be precise with the facts and details, I understand that there may be errors and omissions and I pray to my Guru, Lord Muruga and my readers to forgive me for such errors.

Rahul Kabade

Table of Contents

SKANDA PURANA AND SRI MURUGAN

!!Om Gam Ganapathaye Namaha!!

!! Om Sharavana Bhava !!

India is the holy land of deities and divinities. As it is with any deity or divine presence in Hindu scriptures, Murugan is an omnipotent god whose glorious history can be traced back through multiple Hindu scriptures. The Vedas and Puranas have different interpretations about how Murugan came into being, and if literature is included as evidence for his wonderful and awe-inspiring incarnation, then the historical accounts only increase in number. However, what remains clear is the essence of his birth and subsequent endeavors leading to the common belief through the Hindu religion (Sanatana dharma) that anyone who prays to Murugan and fasts on specified days (specially Fridays) shall have all his wishes granted and sins pardoned.

The objective here is not to contest historical accuracy or present only one account, where there are different versions, but to capture the most important stories and their significance and meaning in everyday life and in Murugan worship. What can be summarized from all ancient scriptures is this: Murugan is the son of Lord Shiva and Devi Parvati. This is a fact we find in various scriptures, and here in this text will be found the most complete story possible of Murugan.

It is important to mention the Trimurti (three forms) or Great Trinity in Hinduism to place in perspective the legend of Muruga. The Trinity comprises of gods Brahma, Vishnu and Shiva. The cosmic functions of creation, maintenance, and destruction are personified by Brahma the creator, Vishnu the maintainer or sustainer or preserver, and Shiva the destroyer or transformer.

The names Muruga (or Muruka) and Murugan are used interchangeably, Muruga being the more personal and loving way to address Him, whereas Murugan being the more reverential tone.

Amongst the many deities present in the Hindu tradition, the birth and life of Murugan is the most complicated one to analyze. He is not only known by different names but also worshipped in different forms in different traditions. He was present during the Rig Veda and is worshipped by both Brahmins and tribals with equal fervor. For simplicity we will use Murugan to refer to Him throughout this book, although various deeds and events give him different names during his various incarnations which may not concur with the practice of bestowing one name.

The Puranas are revered and holy ancient religious texts full of tales and descriptions of great Hindu gods and goddesses. Each Purana highlights a specific deity and brings forth for the reader a wonderful meaning about the deity, their names, acts, virtues, and deeds. The Skanda Purana is but one of the Eighteen Puranas.

'*Purana*' means 'ancient tales,' and traditionally they were used to explain the Vedas to the common people. Ancient legends about sages, kings and heroes were recorded for the benefit of the commoner. Though most of the ancient Puranas are now extinct, the ones written by Sage Veda Vyasa are available to this day.

The Puranas explain the importance of compassion, charity, sacrifice, and virtuous deeds. They also explain the greatness of literature, music, dance and architecture in detail. Reading the Puranas also gives a glimpse of the everyday life of ancient India, allowing the culture, religion and ethics of the time to be understood as well.

The study of the Vedas (Sanskrit vid = 'to know') without the study of the Puranas is akin to studying the body without studying the soul or its essence. The Puranas are referred to as the 'self' or soul (in Sanskrit the '*atman*') of the Vedas and Upanishads. Hence, the study of the Vedas and Upanishads is incomplete without the study of the Puranas. Upanishad in

Sanskrit means "to sit down near a teacher or person" as was the method of instruction in ancient times.

The most renowned ancient Hindu scripture is the Mahabharata, which was composed by the great Sage Veda Vyasa. His mother was Devi Satyavati and his father was Parashara. He was the grandparent of the Kauravas and Pandavas of Mahabharata. Mahabharata was his first composition, followed by the Vedas and Puranas. He was called Veda Vyasa, as he took the Vedas and partitioned them. 'Vyasa' means 'partitioning.' He is believed in the Hindu tradition to be an immortal and still lives on as a Chiranjeev (one with a long life). He first composed 100,000 shlokas (verses or couplets) and then added another 400,000 verses. These came to be known as the Mahapuranas ('maha' meaning 'great' or 'major'). The festival of Guru Pournima (Guru means preceptor or teacher or one who dispels darkness of spiritual ignorance) is dedicated to this master as the day of having partitioned the Vedas into four parts. The tradition of offering puja (prayers) to one's guru in expression of gratitude now translates into every aspect of Hindu tradition, wherever a student pays respect to his/her teacher, be it any field, whether of any art or science.

Any Purana is defined by five characteristics, which are: the creation of the universe, the cyclicity of nature and creation, the numerous aeons or eras, the solar and lunar dynasties, and their descendants.

The Puranas categories are based on the three qualities of the universe and the respective trinity gods which symbolize these: Sattvic, Rajasic and Tamasic. Puranas which glorify Vishnu (the preserver) are Sattvic, those which extoll Brahma (the creator) are Rajasic, and those which describe and worship Shiva (the destructor of ego in the Shaivite tradition) are Tamasic. Skanda Purana falls under the Tamasic category. This should not be confused with the Skanda Upapurana (minor or supplementary) or *Kanda Purana* which is focused on Murugan and his ascent. The Skanda Purana was composed from various scattered or fragmented texts and, hence, does not exist as one complete body.

The Skanda Purana describes the story of Lord Shiva's son, Skanda, who is also known as Karthikeyan, Subrahmanya, Shanmukha, Murugan, and many more names. The legendary poet Kalidasa composed the Kumarasambhava based on the Skanda Purana.

There are two variations of the origin of Skanda Purana. One school of thought believes that it was originally narrated by goddess Parvati to her son, Murugan, who later passed it to Nandi (attendant of Lord Shiva), and subsequently to Sage Atri.

The other explanation is that Murugan (incarnated as Skanda), himself narrated it to Sage Bhrigu, and it was then passed in succession by recital to sages such as Angira, Chyawana and Richika. Sage Veda Vyasa took these fragments and put them together to form the present-day Skanda Purana. The Skanda Purana narrates the stories of the Tatpurusha Kalpa.

To explain the concept of Kalpa it would help to first understand the time scales as mentioned in the Vedas. At present as of today, the current Lord Brahma is in his first day of his 51st year of age. One day span of twenty four hours of Lord Brahma consists of two Kalpas, one night kalpa and other day Kalpa. The first fifty years of Brahma were known as the first Parardha. Hence, we are now in the Dvitiya (second) Parardha.

The current Kalpa is called *Shveta Varaha* Kalpa. In this Kalpa, six Manavantaras have elapsed and we are in the seventh Manavantara. The present Manavantara is called Vaivasvatha Manavantara (or Sraddhadeva Manavantara).

In the present day Vaivasvatha Manavantara, twenty seven Mahayugas have elapsed. One Mahayuga comprises of four Yugas — the Satya (or Krita or enlightened era), Treta, Dwapara and Kali Yuga (dark ages). We are presently in the twenty eighth Mahayuga of which the first three Yugas have passed. Hence, we are in the Kali Yuga of the twenty eighth Mahayuga.

Our present day Kali Yuga began at midnight on the 17th/18th day of the month of February in the year 3102 BC according to the proleptic Julian calendar. Hence, in the year 2012 we are in 5114 year of the present Kali Yuga. Based on this calendar the time elapsed since the task of creation has been started by the current Brahma in the cosmic cycle is roughly 155.52 Trillion years. The Satya or Krita Yuga lasts for four times 432,000 years, Treta lasts for three times 432,000 years, Dwapara is two times 432,000 years and Kali Yuga lasts for 432,000 years.

In Tatpurusha Kalpa, Brahma's son, Daksha Prajapati, had wedded his daughter, Dakshayani, to Shiva. However, Daksha Prajapati was not happy with Shiva, as he sought respect, which he did not get. So he started slandering Shiva. He arranged a sacrificial fire ceremony (*Yagna*), in which he invited all the sages and gods; however, he specifically did not invite his daughter and Shiva. When Dakshayani came to know about the *Yagna*, she pleaded with Shiva to attend. However, Shiva did not wish to go without an invitation and reluctantly agreed that Dakshayani go instead.

At the *Yagna*, a portion of the benefit of offerings is traditionally made in a highly respectful manner to Shiva; however, Daksha Prajapati again publicly slandered Shiva at this event. Dakshayani could not bear the abuse of Shiva, and immolated herself with the fire of *Yagna*. Shiva's attendants, including Virabhadra (the one with three eyes and a thousand arms) landed at the *Yagna* and destroyed everything. Sages like Bhrigu and Pusha were humiliated and most participants were slaughtered. Virabhadra beheaded Daksha and threw his head into fire.

Brahma pleaded and prayed to Shiva to intervene. In his infinite mercy, Shiva restored the *Yagna*; however, as Daksha's head was already burnt and could not be restored, a goat's head was planted on Daksha's body and he was brought back to life by Shiva. Hereafter Daksha transformed and became a devotee of Lord Shiva.

The loss of Dakshayani caused Shiva severe grief, and he went into deep meditation for thousands of years. Shiva's absence caused evil and demons to plague earth and the demon Taraka (aka Tarakasuran), who was the son of Maya, became powerful. He performed penance to please Brahma and asked for a boon of immortality. However, Brahma could not give such a boon to any, as it was against the law of prakriti (Mother Nature). So he offered Tarakasuran a boon wherein his death became next to impossible. Tarakasuran thought that Shiva has gone into meditation for thousands of years and that there was no possibility of Shiva remarrying again, so he asked that he should die only at the hand of Shiva's son. Brahma agreed and granted him this boon. Tarakasuran became more and more powerful and started abusing human beings and the gods and goddesses with his powers and the near-impossibility of his death. He defeated the devatas (or Deva — used to refer to God or various individuals who display His power; Sanskrit Deev means 'lustre' or 'to play') and drove them out of heaven in a battle.

The devatas beseeched Brahma for a solution, to which he guided them. Following his direction, they then appealed to Mount Himalaya and his wife, Mena, who had a girl child called by various names such as Uma, Gouri and Parvati for a rescue. Parvati was a rebirth of Dakshayani. From the age of eight, she was taken by her father to a place where Shiva used to meditate. Parvati tried all possible means of praying to Shiva to win him as her husband; however, all her efforts were negated by Shiva.

The devatas then plotted and prayed to Kamadeva or Madana (the god who carries the bow and arrow of love, similar to Cupid) to intervene to make this union possible. Kamadeva intervened and showered his arrows on Shiva, and turned his hermitage into a beautiful garden with fragrant flowers. This disturbed Shiva's meditation. When Shiva came out of his meditation, he was greeted with Parvati holding a garland and Kamadeva with his bow and arrow. Shiva was enraged and furious about the disruption, and fire came out from his third eye and burnt Kamadeva to ashes. He left the hermitage and Parvati was completely distraught. However, she did not give up, despite her parents forcing her to leave her dream of having Shiva as her husband.

Thereafter Parvati performed severe penance, so much so that she gave up drinking water and would not even eat a Parna (leaf). Hence, she came to be known as Aparna. Shiva was finally pleased with her penance, but he wanted to test Parvati in every possible way. He appeared to her in disguise and slandered Shiva. He would ask her, "What would such a young and beautiful girl like Parvati gain from marrying Shiva? Shiva is a wanderer, covered with ashes, wearing a garland of skulls and moving around with spirits and ghosts in cremation grounds and who could never keep her happy." Parvati was angry with the criticism of Shiva and she asked this person to go away, saying there was no need for him to be talking nonsense about Shiva.

Shiva was finally pleased to reveal his true form to Parvati and agreed to a marriage. Shiva was married with pomp and ceremony to Parvati, and the married couple left for Mount Gandhamadana. Then, the couple was lost for thousands of years with Nandi (the bull on which Lord Shiva rides also represents virility and strength) guarding the doorway. With the continued absence of Shiva and Parvati, the devatas grew worried as they were expecting a child to be born who would kill the demon Tarakasuran.

Brahma, Vishnu and the devatas now plotted to spy on Shiva. They sent Agni (the god of fire) to find out what was happening. Agni contracted his body and tricked Nandi. He reached the inner confines of Shiva and Parvati's chamber and was spotted spying by Shiva. Shiva was enraged and while incomplete in his union with Parvati, his third eye opened and six rays of fire leapt towards Agni. Only Agni could bear the heat of Shiva's fire, though not for long, so he was forced to accept it. [As Skanda Purana has two significantly differing accounts of Murugan's birth, the more commonly-accepted version is presented here]. The unbearable heat and strength of the rays from Shiva's eyes were damaging to Agni. He prayed to Vishnu for deliverance, and Vishnu, in turn, advised him to pray to Shiva for mercy. Because of his pleading, Shiva asked Agni to use the intense blazing energy to relieve the cold from those who were suffering in winter. So Agni went to a lake and waited. At this lake the wives of the *Saptarishis* (seven sages — the earliest sacred text Jaiminiya Brahmana lists the seven sages as Vashistha, Bharadwaja, Jamadagni, Gautama, Atri, Vishvamitra, and Agastya.) came for an early morning bath. As it was very cold, Agni offered them the warmth of the fire, which they gladly accepted, except for Arundhati (wife of Vashistha), who thought it to be improper. In offering the warmth of fire, Agni relieved himself of Shiva's energy, as it had now entered the bodies of six wives of the *rishis* ('seer' to whom the Vedas were *'originally revealed'*).

When the *Saptarishis* came to know about this, they cursed their wives to be born as stars. This paved the way for the wives to become *krittikas* (Pleiades). Before they became stars, however, they released the energy of Shiva on top of Mount Himalaya, and this scattered energy (Skanna) floated down the Ganges to a pond of reeds (shara) alongside the river.

From Skanna originates the name Skanda. In this pond of reeds (sharavana) was born a baby with six faces and twelve arms. This was Murugan. As he had six (shada) faces (anana), he was called Shadanana or Shanmukha. As he was born of the Ganges, he was named Gangeya. As he was born of the six krittikas (Pleiades), he was named Karthikeya by Sage Garga. Parvati felt in her heart that she had mothered a child, and Sage Narada brought the news of the birth of Murugan. Both Shiva and Parvati came to this pond, filled with joy, and Parvati lifted the six-faced child and pressed it to her bosom. At that precise moment, the six faces merged into a beautiful child. Murugan is thus said to be born of the bosoms of Parvati. Shiva took Murugan in his arms, and baby Murugan played with the snake around Shiva's neck. The devatas were filled with joy at this event, as their savior was born.

In the second interpretation, which is similar to the one in Mahabharata, the birth of Murugan is from Agni and his wife Swaha. In this story, Agni is smitten by the beauty of the wives of *Saptarishis*, so his wife, Swaha, assumes the form of these wives and unites with Agni six times. Swaha then takes the energy generated during these unions and places them in a golden pit of reeds on six occasions. Swaha could not assume the form of Arundhati due to her devoutness and purity. Later, the boy Murugan is born in this golden pit of reeds on Mount Shweta.

There are distinct similarities in the accounts of Sanskrit (North Indian) literature and Sangam (South Indian) literature with that of the Puranas, except that the asura, or evil demi-god in the story, was Surapadman (as opposed to Tarakasuran). However, stories of war with Tarakasuran and Surapadman are covered here. Most of the other aspects of this historical recount of Murugan's birth remain true. Another addition to the story suggests that Murugan became the leader of the demi-god army on Earth after marrying Devasena, the daughter of Lord Indra (king of devatas), to lead the devatas to a victory over Surapadman. Lord Sri Krishna states in Srimad Bhagavatam that, among Generals, He is also the commander in chief of the army of devatas as Skanda (wartime incarnation of Murugan).

Maya was a woman of the daitya or asura clan and she attracted Sage Kashyapa. The asuras Surapadman, Simhamukhan, Tarakasuran and Ajamukhi were born from this union. From the sweat of these asuras, hundreds of thousands of other asuras were born. Surapadman and his younger brothers studied under the Sage Shukracharya. They both performed severe penance towards Lord Shiva for many years.

Lord Shiva pleased with their penance appeared before Surapadman and granted him the power to live for a hundred and eight Yugas, to rule a thousand and eight kingdoms and to be undefeatable even by the forces of Lord Vishnu.

Surapadman could only be killed when the power created by Indra's chariot, the Lion throne and four other forces were joined together. Surapadman and his soldiers invaded heaven and burned it. They enslaved devatas and made them do household cleaning chores. Ajamukhi was sent to kidnap Indra's wife and Surapadman asked his son Bhanugopan to burn heaven. He imprisoned the son of Indra and treated the devatas harshly.

Battle with Surapadman

The Puranas (with their hidden meanings explained in the form of stories) are instructive texts to help mankind lead a socially responsible life and a personal life of joy, peace and happiness. All stories have two layers of meaning: one, the actual story told and two, the symbolization or hidden meaning of various facts. The Skanda Purana narrates one such war story of Murugan with Surapadman and his brothers.

Though the story has different versions, (from Shiva's penance to the clever boon that Surapadman obtains) Murugan's birth is no ordinary one. After he is made the commander-in-chief of the celestial army Devi Parvati presents him with his most powerful weapon, the Shakti Vel (powerful spear).

After leading the celestial army to victory over the brothers (and many followers) of Surapadman, the chief of devatas and the chief of asuras meet for the final battle. It is said they travelled the three universes fighting each other for four days. Surapadman who learned many magical tricks from his mother Maya employed these illusions against his enemies. He awakened the dead asuras and also rode a magical chariot with the head of a lion. He also assumed various forms of birds and animals with the help of the *mantras* (sounds capable of creating transformation) that he had learned from his Guru Shukracharya. Shukracharya used the *Sanjivani Vidya* to bring back the dead asuras to life.

Shukracharya a Bhargava *rishi* is the son of Sage Bhrigu and the guru of asuras. He is identified with planet Venus and presides over the day of Friday (Shukravar). However, he is also cited as the son of Kavyamata (Kavya). Bhrigu's wife was Puloma. Their son was named Kavi. However, there is no mention of Kavi's wife. He studied under *rishi* Angira (aka Angirasa). But Angira always favored his own son, Brihaspati

(Guru of devatas) which disturbed Shukracharya and became the cause of his enmity with the devatas. He was a devout Shiva devotee. It is said that he performed intense penance by hanging upside down from a tree for a thousand years to earn a boon from Shiva of *Sanjivani Vidya*. *Sanjivani* is the formula or medicine to revive the dead back to life. His enmity with devatas also stems from his hatred of Lord Vishnu who had killed his mother Kavyamata who had sheltered some asuras. Shukracharya did revive his mother back to life using *Sanjivani*.

But Murugan in his battle with Surapadman and Shukracharya's tricks employed the special weapon given by his father for this very purpose—the Pashupatastra. With one swipe of the astra (weapon), Murugan sent all the awakened asuras back to the nether-land. He also used another weapon that brought the magical chariot of Surapadman to his own use. Surapadman then assumed the form of the huge bird Chaksavaham, but Murugan employed Indra as a peacock and cut the bird into two.

With the battle reaching its peak, and Surapadman deprived of his brothers, his army and his weapons, he cunningly assumed the form of a tree. Murugan threw his vel which split the tree into two. Thus Surapadman was cut into two and one half became Murugan's vehicle, the peacock, and the other became a rooster, Murugan's banner emblem.

On the surface, the fight seems to be between good and evil but it has a deeper meaning. Surapadman and his brothers Simhamukhan and Tarakasuran were the sons of Maya. They represent the three gunas (characters or modes of Mother Nature) that one has to overcome to achieve union with the Supreme. They are Tamas, Rajas and Sattva gunas. The *Jiva* (soul) is under the influence of these three gunas that prevent it from reaching the inner self (God). Murugan destroys these three to help an individual on its journey.

The mount of Murugan is the beautiful peacock which is the only bird that can reveal its joy by dancing. Murugan sitting on the peacock represents the conquest over glory and beauty of Maya. For a huge bird with slim legs, a peacock's balance is perfect. It symbolizes the mental balance needed to attain contentment and happiness in life. The bird is perched on a snake, this represents that Murugan has control over serpents e.g., the malefic effects of the planet Rahu (son of Maya). Mental tranquility is important for gaining knowledge of life and the universe. The cock banner of Murugan has its own significance because it symbolizes the dawn of knowledge. A cock always proclaims the rising Sun early in the morning. This story shows that Murugan can liberate the soul from the clutches of illusion and free it from evil forces.

VARIOUS NAMES OF SRI MURUGAN

As with most deities and gods in the Hindu scriptures, Murugan is also blessed with many wonderful names. In Subrahmanya Ashtottara, Murugan is remembered by chanting 108 beautiful names. Many of the names are commonly used as Tamil and Malayalam baby names. There are many more names bestowed upon Murugan but most of the names are either synonyms of the below explained names or they signify a similar contextual meaning.

One might find it confusing that one Hindu god is known by a thousand different names. There are a multitude of reasons for this. The most important reason being that the names signify some greatness or incarnation or event which benefited humankind and they are easy to remember due to a glorious meaning or tale behind it. With millions of devotees and each with a differing temperament, god becomes personalized to each person in a form or a name that is nearest to that devotee's heart.

Murugan

The literal translation of the Tamil word "Murugan" means beauty or beautiful one. Skanda is called Murugan because of his everlasting beauty and youthful appearance. As explained earlier, being born from the bosoms of Devi Parvati and the fire from the third eye of Lord Shiva, Murugan truly possesses the youthfulness of Lord Shiva and the splendid beauty of Devi Parvati.

Since Lord Murugan appeared for a special and specific purpose on this earth the three eternal divine functions of the world are contained in his very name MURUKA. The first letter of his name MU stands for Mukundan or Vishnu who is Sthithi (protection) RU is Rudra (Shiva) and stands for Samharan (destruction) and KA for Kamalan or Brahma the Srishti (creation).

His name also means honey, fragrance, and eternal youth and his name Murugan exudes his charm, beauty and grace on millions of his devotees. Murugan also has other esoteric meanings, He is known as 'Vizhikki Thunai' (guide to the eyes) or the one who opens our eyes to the reality of the world. Murugan provides the inner vision to lead a life of bliss and peace.

As Karthikeya, he is the fearless leader of the army against evil forces and by just chanting his name obstacles can be overcome in life. The 'moola mantra' (main mantra) of Om Saravana Bhava holds the six aspects of life in it. By chanting the mantra we can experience the energy of Skanda. While SA is the ability to attract people, RA is for bringing prosperity into life. VA is meant to remove physical discomforts, competitions and debts. NA is used to overcome obstacles presented by enemies, while BA brings charm and finally VA represents the end of all evil forces.

But the name of Lord Murugan is also evoked in esoteric forms when he's called to be the 'guide' of life. When we call on Murugan to be 'Mozhikki Thunai' (guide to language) it means we need his help in getting rid of our language of ego. We need his help in rising above petty pride and prejudices and learn to speak the language of truth. Who can be a better guide in this than the god of wisdom and truth? Murugan also teaches us to speak politely, clearly and gently, He also teaches us the importance of silence.

Murugan is also known as 'Pazhikki Thunai' (guide of deeds) by saying the name of Murugan we can be liberated from the cycle of birth. The 'karma' or the consequences of our actions is eliminated by constantly reciting the various names of Murugan.

When we call upon Murugan to be our 'Vazhikki Thunai' (guide to a path) we make Him our guide in life. No matter what paths we may take in a lifetime, with Murugan as a guide we reach our final destination with peace.

By saying the name of Murukan, six gods are evoked—MU stands for Mukundan — Vishnu, and Lakshmi lives in Vishnu's heart. RU is for Rudran, and Shakti is always known as half of

Shiva. KA for Brahma and Saraswati resides in Brahma's tongue. Murugan is also known as the '*Jnana Pundita*' (jnana means knowledge inseparable from experience of 'total reality', Pundita means a learned person or an expert) or the source of all knowledge; he enlightens the world with his presence since he emerged from the '*jyoti*' (light) of Lord Shiva. His own father Lord Shiva—the Supreme ruler of the world—had to become his disciple once, to accept the power of Murugan's knowledge.

Murugan the 'Karunakaran' (merciful Lord) represents the virtues of love and compassion. When he pardoned the demon Surapadman and made him his vehicle instead of completely destroying him, he showed his devotees his magnanimity and mercy. Even today just observing a simple vrata (observance or fast) is enough to seek his divine blessings.

Murugan as 'Guhan'—the word 'Guha' means cave and, Lord Murugan as Guhan dwells in the 'caves' (hearts) of his devotees. He is the inner-controller of all emotions and when we call him Guhan he resides in our hearts removing all darkness from within. Most of the hymns sung praising Skanda start with 'glory to him who illuminates the hearts'.

Murugan as 'Azaghan' (beauty) shows that inner beauty should first be achieved, to manifest the outer beauty. He resides in the soul of his devotee as a beautiful and magnificent god that removes ignorance at all levels. In Thiruppugazh a hymn was written by his ardent devotee, Sri Arunagirinathar which says that even four-thousand eyes are not enough to behold the exquisite beauty of the Lord. Thiruppugazh songs are sung by Murugan devotees even today with the same fervor, and Murugan manifests his knowledge, mercy and beauty in all true seekers to this day.

Kanta or Kanthan

This Sanskrit word literally translates to 'the beloved'. It is more commonly used to refer to Lord Vishnu as it is mentioned twice in the Vishnu Sahasranama. However, it is also used to describe Murugan for his divine nature because of which everything around us is possible. As explained by Aadi Shankaracharya, Brahma the creator is also referred to as 'Ka'. 'Anta' literally translates to 'end' and its Sanskrit meaning is 'putting an end to' means the Supreme Being who can end creation during his withdrawal from sustenance in the cosmic cycle.

Kanthan pronounced as Kaanta is a name given to Lord Muruga, due to his incredible beauty that stems from inner perfection. He is the beautiful one and the most precious one to his devotees.

Blessed with perfection from his parents, Murugan is the most loved deity among Tamilians (both in India and Sri Lanka) and hence, dearly referred to as Lord Kanthan.

Karthikeyan or Karthigeyan

Murugan is commonly referred to by this name for two reasons:

Being born from the combination (or joining) of six babies under the care of six Karthigai (Krittikai) maidens, he is called Karthigai Swami. *Krittika* is the open star cluster 'Pleiades' in Indian astrology. The literal meaning of Karthikeyan or Karthika or Karthiga is 'The giver of courage and happiness'.

Karthik is the eight month in the Hindu lunar calendar. It corresponds to October—November of the solar calendar with the sun sign of babies being born during this period being Scorpio.

Karthigeyan translated means an embodiment of bravery and faith who conquered all obstacles using his powerful spear— the vel—and used his devotion to the Father and Mother of the Universe to battle doubt and other distractions of the world. Spiritually, the word is associated with the action of refraining from worldly needs and desires, fighting inner evils and spirits to overcome them with bravery and then live eternally in bliss.

Rahul Kabade

Saravanabhava or Sharavanabhava or Saravana

Not only is this an alternative name for Murugan but also a *mantra* in itself to recall Murugan and his actions; delivering courage, bravery, guidance and enlightenment. The literal translation of the word is a pond surrounded by reeds. It refers to the place of birth of Murugan amidst a forest (vana) in a pond of reeds (shara).

The significance of SHA—RA, first two syllables is that they are *Kumarabijas*. Similarly VA—NA are *Shaktibijas* and BHA—VA are *Shivabijas*.

This means by chanting the *mantra*, Lord Murugan as in Kumara is invoked. In very simple terms *mantras* are the devata itself.

'*Bija*' means a seed and *Bija mantra* is usually of one syllable, for example, Om, Shrim, Hrim, Krim, Hum, Aim, Phat, Krom, Swaha, Klim, Gam etc. are one syllable *mantras*. The absolute supreme exists in every human being as *Jivatma* (*Jiva* means living entity and *atma* or *atman* means the cosmic self or soul) in the form of sound. The heard or uttered *mantra* is the manifestation of the subtle sound of a specific divinity (either male, female or neutral). *Mantras* themselves are the forms of Kundalini that reside in the *chakras* (nerve plexuses) in a

33

human being. The six *chakras* being Mooladhara near genitalia, Svadhishthana located near lower abdomen, Anahata in the heart, Vishuddhi in the throat, Ajna located between the eyebrows and Sahasrara at the top of the head-crown. Some belief systems also include a seventh chakra the Manipura chakra located near the navel. By chanting the *mantras* one energizes the *chakras* which in turn vitalize the physical, emotional and the spiritual wellbeing.

A more popular meaning for Saravana Bhava is that it is the embodiment of all five elements of the universe and the spirit of Lord Shiva that was inculcated distinctly during the birth of Murugan. The deities Agni, Vayu, Ganga, Mother Earth (Dharti) and Devi Parvati represent each of the five elements that make up Murugan.

Shanmukha or Shanmughan

The name Shanmukha means 'six faces' and it is obvious why this name is linked with Murugan. He is the six-faced god. The six sparks that came out of Shiva's third eye became Aarumughan, (One with six faces) and while the first five faces represent the five elements—fire, water, earth, air and space, the sixth face of Murugan represents the spirit that gives life to beings that are formed from the five fundamental elements.

Each face of Murugan also has a specific function; while one face fulfills the desires of his devotees; another face removes ignorance and bestows knowledge. A third face of Murugan brings out the inner secrets, while the fourth face gives strength and inspiration to perform sacrifices and rituals. The fifth face of Murugan is to protect the good and punish the bad. The sixth face of Murugan ignites unconditional love for the divine and gives happiness to seekers.

The human body has six *chakras* (centers of power) located throughout, and the six heads of Murugan symbolically represent those six vital centers. Only by concentrating on these *chakras* and 'awakening' them, can human beings sublimate their base nature. The state of '*sat-chit-ananda*' (existence-knowledge-absolute-bliss) can be attained by true devotion to Lord Murugan.

Apart from the six faces Murugan also has twelve hands that work in tandem to help and protect his devotees. He also has his Shakti Vel, (powerful spear) that both protects the devotees from evil and destroys ignorance so the soul can journey to its original form of pristine glory. Murugan's vehicle, (the peacock) and his emblem, (the rooster) help devotees overcome the Maya (illusion) of life so the path to god-realization becomes clear. With so many attributes it is no wonder that Murugan attracts devotees from various walks of life.

Skanda

There are a few stories woven around this single name for Murugan. The scattered energy deposited by Swaha in the golden pits of Mount Shweta led to the birth of Murugan, hence the name Skanda (Skanna means discharged or scattered). Skanda in Sanskrit means spurting or flowing or 'leaping out' and as mentioned in the legend previously that Lord Shiva could not complete his union with Devi Parvati and his energy (seed) leapt out, which was later carried by Agni, hence the name Skanda.

Subrahmanya

This name is bestowed upon Murugan to signify his divine power over all mortal beings and souls. 'Su' in Sanskrit means anything that is good and 'Brahmanya' means one who has realized 'Brahmaan' as in the supreme Universal spirit. It depicts his power of transformation that urged even the asura, Surapadman, to see through the veil of deceit and greed for power so that he could ultimately come to accept the graceful forms of a peacock and a rooster.

Gangeya

The river Ganga originates in the Himalayas (abode of Lord Shiva) and is considered to be the most sacred river to Hindus.

The river is considered as a personification of goddess Ganga and is worshipped as a goddess. One who bathes or soaks in the river is said to rid the accumulated sins of that person of ten lifetimes. Gangeya is an obvious name given to Murugan because of his birth from the river Ganges, who is also graced as Murugan's mother. Ganga in Sanskrit means 'swift—goer'.

Velayudha

In reference to the great Lord's choice of weapon, the vel—a powerful spear (gifted to him by his mother, Devi Parvati). It signifies the destruction of the entire asura race as well as metaphorically signifying Murugan's supreme knowledge—and power to bestow that knowledge — over all his followers who dwell in the unknowing or in ignorance (*ajnana*). Velayudha means the Lord who carries the vel as his weapon.

Guha or Guhan

Murugan is also called Lord Guhan because he is a cave dweller. Cave here means the heart. He dwells amidst the hearts of his followers, lighting the way, guiding them towards supreme knowledge and freeing them of all desires, fulfilling their true wishes. True freedom from desires is not about having choices but being free from the slavery of choices. It is said that Murugan lives in the cave of every person's heart but is most sensitive towards the pain and ecstasy of his followers. It also signifies that the true seat of knowledge finally rests in the heart and not the mind. When one commences Murugan Bhakti, one's viewpoint and outlook changes from outside—in to inside—out. This means that the devotee is transformed and looks at the world from his or her heart.

Swaminathan or Swaminatha

When it came to the knowledge of *Pranava* (the secrets of the soul or OM) no one can possess more knowledge than Murugan as is stated in Puranas. This is one of the most beautiful tales where, due to his unhappiness with the work of creation being handled by Lord Brahma, Murugan imprisons Brahma as Brahma is unable to tell Murugan the exact meaning of the powerful *mantra* "OM".

Upon this, the devatas plead with Lord Shiva for Brahma's release. When Lord Shiva summons Murugan, He is faced with the same question of what is the true meaning of "OM". At this point Murugan becomes the "Guru" of Lord Shiva (His father) and recites the meaning in the ears of Lord Shiva.

Murugan further releases Brahma from prison only to receive a curse from Brahma—that Murugan will be reborn in each Yuga as a snake, (OM being the latent serpentine Kundalini residing in the Mooladhara chakra).

Murugan as Swaminatha here means the guru of the father.

AARU-PADAI VEEDU – THE SIX GREAT ABODES

OF MURUGAN

There are six temples in Tamil Nadu that together form the Aaru-padai Veedu or collection of Murugan's great abodes. They are Swamimalai, Palani, Tiruttani, Thiruparankundram, Pazhamudir Solahi (Cholai) and Tiruchendur. Most Tamil names of gods, places of worship or names of towns and cities start with the word *tiru* or *thiru.* Thiru denotes sacred and has its roots in the Tamil word *'thir'* meaning open, hence *thiru* denotes a place or person from which one can obtain abundance.

Other than these six great abodes, temples for the worship and praise of Murugan are scattered across various parts of the globe. Wherever a Tamil community resides, so shall a Murugan temple find its rightful place. For example, in Sri Lanka there are two main temples for Murugan, namely: Nallur Kandaswamy Temple at Jaffna and Kadirkama Skanda Temple at Kadirkama (Kathirgama). In Malaysia, one shall find the Murugan Temple near Kuala Lumpur at the Batu caves. There are a few more in London, Australia, Singapore and Mauritius.

Days of Worship

There are many days considered quite auspicious for the worship of Murugan. I am covering three of these here. Thaipusam is one of the most important festivals for Murugan, celebrated during the months of January to February. It is said that on this day, Murugan accepted the vel, his most powerful weapon from his mother, Devi Parvati to destroy the asura demons.

Another festival associated with Subrahmanya is Skanda Shashti celebrated for a period of six days during the Tamil month of Aippasi (during October – November). During this six-day period, fasting is observed and prayers are offered to Murugan. Also, in the Month of May to June on a full-moon day, the birth of Murugan is celebrated. It is called the Vaikaasi Visaakam.

A detailed note on the celebration of Agni Nakshatram and of Murugan abhishekam (bathing an idol) is covered separately in this book.

Murugan is also worshipped as Nature. The worship of Murugan is considered the same as the worship of nature (Prakriti). He is glorified as the most beautiful of all sentient and mortal beings, the feeling of grace, the blessings of the gods, and the embodiment of nature. Just as nature is all around us and its scenic beauty inspires pure visions, dreams and purity within us, the praise of Murugan brings forth feelings of divinity, wisdom and grace within us. Clearly then, Murugan has been rightfully associated with Mother Nature.

Understanding Murugan Worship

South India and Sri Lanka are two places that witness a great deal of Murugan worship. Murugan is so popular in these parts of the world that almost every town in the south displays its affection and acceptance through a temple dedicated to the worship of Murugan.

Before one can engage in the worship of Murugan, one must understand what Murugan shall grant to his believers and why he would grant the same. For this, his birth (and subsequent life) provides all the answers. Remember that one of our stories mentioned that he was the culmination of six different babies spread upon red lotus leaves that emerged as a result of emanations from Lord Shiva's Ajna Chakra (or, the third eye). This in itself tells us what Murugan signifies. He signifies the accumulation of all knowledge and wisdom in the world, not the material kind that brings momentary relief but the truly divine that feels ephemeral and blessed.

When Murugan was born from the bosoms and due to the grace of Devi Parvati, which united the six babies, he is said to have achieved the state of *Purna* (perfection or completeness). It is the same as the complete alignment of the soul, body and spirit with the single-most important truth: Murugan is supreme when it comes to *jnana* or wisdom. Achieving his grace alone shall mean the complete annihilation of darkness, destruction of *ajnana*. However, attaining Murugan's grace is not easy. His worship is a task that requires a rigorous study and understanding of the Skanda Purana.

Before you can ask Murugan for a wish, you have to qualify yourself to Him. The devatas did not simply come up to Murugan and ask for help, they first qualified themselves to be worthy of Murugan's grace and only then did they ask for his support in victory. The process of making oneself worthy of god's attention is called *Daivi Prakriti* (of godly nature) or becoming an *adhikari* (rightful or worthy). It requires you to realize that Murugan shall grant only to those whom he sees fit.

No worship of Murugan is complete if it is not done in true alignment with the teachings of the Skanda Purana. The first clue as to how Murugan's grace can be achieved comes from the devatas incessant struggle against the asuras. Time and again, the devatas were defeated in their battle with the evil-doers even when they stood on the side of the good; but they never gave up. They recognized that there was a force which was evil and that it stood against the good. They took arms against it, decided to fight it, and continued to do so until they had tried everything. It was only after they exhausted all their efforts (and then fought on some more) that they actually did approach Murugan, the truly beautiful one. It was the devatas *true* struggle, their complete surrender to Murugan and their willingness to accept that there was an opposing force that needed destruction which led them to seek out Murugan's grace and attain ultimate victory.

A worshipper of Murugan must first acknowledge the truth in their requests; find out what plagues them within, what causes them unrest and what evil ideas clog their being. Only after recognizing all these complications within themselves should the worshipper continue with the prayers. Taking clues from the devatas struggle we see that simple recognition is not enough. As humans we must accept our deepest evil secrets and fight against them time and again. Yes, that evil will emerge victorious more often than we want, but we must never give in to defeat and submission when faced with *ajnana*, that is, ignorance of the fact that god resides within us and we are truly and originally divine. The only form of submission that we should show through our struggle with *ajnana* is in front of Murugan, the supreme knower of truth.

By doing so we are making ourselves surrender to the universal ego or the conscience of Murugan instead of submitting to our personal ego. Our personal ego is made up of lower energies that drag us down and produce evil thoughts in our mind. It is the act of true worship; prayers and *vratas* (penances) practiced over time through *abhyasa* (study) that we can ultimately annihilate *ajnana* within us and bring out the godliness that makes us bow down before the Supreme from within. At this moment, our wishes are answered by Murugan for he takes the place of our self as we fade into the background. We then become one and the same with god, seeking his blessings and receiving them in earnest. Murugan shall take charge of our personality and we shall become resigned with glory and peace to his will—the will of the divine.

To achieve the grace and wisdom of Murugan, one must also engage in some sadhana's or *vratas* (a penance such as fasting, or prayer) that form an integral part of any Hindu belief system. No ritual or festival goes without a proper set of observances to strictly follow. The observances that are required to be followed during the worship of Murugan were proposed long ago by Sage Vashistha to King Muchukunda. He laid down three methods of offering worship to Murugan.

The first method of worship was supposedly used by another King Bhagirathi to conquer his foe, Gora. He observed fasting every Friday for three years in a row, at the end of which his wish for success in battle with Gora came true. It is said that observing a fast after a ritualized bath on Friday is the most auspicious of all rituals for the appeasement of Murugan.

In the second method one must maintain a fast throughout the entire Karthikai day that falls around the end of the Karthik month of the Hindu calendar. By observing this for twelve years in a row, a normal mortal can achieve the heights or become an adhikari (becoming a *deserved*) just as Sage Narada did and became the greatest of all *rishis*.

The third and final method propounded by the Sage is a vrata (fast) to be maintained starting from the day after Dipawali or Diwali (festival of lights) extending through six days till the end of the auspicious period. The vrata requires one to maintain a complete fast throughout the entire duration. However, the Sage also pointed out that those who fail to maintain complete fast may take food once a day and then fast completely on the last day coinciding with the *Shukla Paksha* (brightest fortnight) succeeding the *Prathama Tithi* (first auspicious occasion) or the day of Diwali.

Worship has always been fervent for Murugan in Southern India throughout the regions of Tamil Nadu and Kerala, but, prior to the medieval periods, Murugan worship was also frequently heard of through Northern India specifically in the regions that are presently the states of Haryana, Punjab, West Bengal, Orissa, Maharashtra and Karnataka.

The earliest archeological records point to the Gupta dynasty having close ties with Murugan. Coins, and sculptures depicting Murugan in his traditional warrior pose, have been uncovered from ancient burial grounds belonging to the Gupta period. In fact, many rulers from their time were given names that literally translated to depictions of Murugan himself. This traditional method of worship of Murugan continued well into the next millennia. During post-medieval times, however, Murugan fell out of favor owing to a shift in belief towards Lord Shiva and Devi Parvati. There are still festivals scattered in these regions of northern India that provide a glimpse of what it was like back in those days. Witnessing any of the festivals or pujas conducted in the ancient Murugan temples of the north brings back nostalgic memories for true believers.

Outside India, worship of Murugan has been vehemently followed and practiced through pockets of Malaysia, Singapore, Thailand, Australia and Germany. It seems that wherever Tamilians go so does Murugan.

IMPORTANT TEMPLES OF MURUGAN

Lord Murugan set foot on many lands in the South during his struggle against the tyranny of the asuras and these are the lands which are still worshipped in his name today. Out of the thousands that were graced with his presence, six have been elevated to the level of Aaru-padai Veedu (the military camps or six battle houses) for Murugan.

Thiruparankundram Subrahmanya Swami Temple

Considered foremost out of the six abodes of Murugan, the Thiruparankundram Subrahmanya Swami Temple is also known simply as Thiruparankundram. It is said by the Saint-poet, Nakkirar, that this is one of the first places where Murugan achieved victory over the evil forces. It is today situated in the Madurai district of Tamil Nadu some four miles out of Madurai on a small hillock.

There are a series of pillared halls (mandapams) that elevate gradually on top of each other making up the entire temple. One of the mandapams is dedicated to the Saint-poet Nakkirar, while the first mandapam shows the marriage of Murugan to Deviyani and a few sculptures of Thiramalai Nayak and Magammal. As one descends from the

48

mandapams, there are caves surrounding the area that depict many divine tales and sagas. A more detailed account of Saint-poet Nakkirar is mentioned in a separate chapter in this book.

The major attraction of the temple are the rock-cut caves that surround the entire region with separate shrines for Lord Shiva, Devi Parvati, Vishnu, Ganapati and many other deities. The temple entrance is splendidly built on forty eight 16th century, Nayaka-period-style pillars each carved artistically with engravings on them. The innermost cave of the shrine is made out of a single rock dated 8th century A.D.

All these caves are only accessible through narrow and dark passages hence making it quite difficult to reach them.

The most distinguished feature of the Thiruparankundram temple is the sculpture of Lord Shiva holding the flag of Rishaba whilst he dances. Such a sculpture is not found anywhere else in India. Another peculiarity of the temple is the image of Nandi standing in bull-head and human-body form behind a few sages. Interestingly enough, this is also the only temple where one can worship Lord Brahma since his idols are never found elsewhere (as it is forbidden to worship Brahma). This is because of a curse from Lord Shiva. According to legend, Brahma and Vishnu were asked to find the end of a giant, infinite, fiery pillar that emanated from Lord Shiva. Vishnu was sent towards the bottom and Brahma towards the top. Brahma lied that he had found the top and hence incurred the wrath of Lord Shiva; so much so, in fact, that one of his heads was cut off and he was subjected to a curse stating that Brahma would never be worshipped here on earth. The carriers (vehicles or vahana) for each god, however, are still to be found at the temple, standing side-by-side, right next to one another. Moreover, it is the only temple where the Sun god and Moon god are presented together and worshipped at the same time.

Legend associated with Thiruparankundram

As the mythology goes, Murugan fought alongside the devata army as their General, leading them into victory against Surapadman at Tiruchendur and afterwards set up base camp at Thiruparankundram where celebrations took place everywhere. Lord Indra, pleased with the victory over the asuras, gave Murugan his blessings and also his daughter's hand in marriage. His daughter who is considered to be the princess of the devatas, Deviyani was married at Thiruparankundram amidst guests of both divine *and* mortal presence. The Sun and Moon god, too, attended the marriage ceremony along with Lord Shiva, Devi Parvati and many other gods and goddesses.

To mark the wedding, the grounds were deemed sacred by followers of Murugan, The divine sculptor, Vishwakarma, was

50

given the order to set up a temple with sculptures of all the deities who took part in the wedding for mortals to worship. Since this was the place of Murugan's marriage with Deviyani; all of Murugan's sculptures here only have Deviyani beside him. It is, in fact, the only temple where Murugan is not seen with Valli at all.

Another legend holds that the six sons of the Sage Parashara were cursed to live as fishes in the Sharavana Poigai (sacred marshy pond with reeds) until they prayed fervently to Murugan. Upon hearing that Murugan was to grace Thiruparankundram, the six sons waited for Murugan's blessings and as soon as they were blessed by Him their curse was reversed and they regained human forms and were able to live a normal life once more.

The story surrounding this sacred ground is that, after the defeat of the asura Surapadman, Murugan and his devatas army shifted base from Tiruchendur to Thiruparankundram where at the behest of Lord Indra, he went into wedlock with the graceful Deviyani.

Tiruchendur

This was supposed to be the base camp where the final battle between Lord Skanda and Surapadman was waged. It is said that Murugan sent his messenger Veerabahu to the asura capital, Veera Mahendrapuri, from Tiruchendur and then

Murugan rested here for a few days after winning the final battle.

The temple here is situated along the southern seashore some thirty five miles away from Tirunelvelly. The festival of Skanda Shashti is fervently celebrated in this temple with thousands of Murugan devotees flocking here to observe the strict six-day fast of the Skanda Shashti Vrata with much austerity and faith. Tiruchendur is also known by different names such as Thirucheeralaivai, Jayanthipuram, Thirubhuvana Maadevi and Chathurvedi Mangalam.

Murugan's Presence in Tiruchendur

Murugan is also known as the Kuranji Kaduval (god of the mountains). It is a popular belief in Southern India (and in Tamil Nadu in particular) that if there is a hill or mountain in any place, Murugan will have a temple there.

According to the Skanda Purana, Murugan was born to destroy the three asuras: Surapadman, Simhamukhan and Tarakasuran. In esoteric terms, the three asuras represent the three vices human beings have to overcome in order to attain union with the divine. Ignorance, ego and karma can only be overcome by praying to Murugan in his various aspects.

The Tiruchendur Temple is the only temple that is located near a seashore rather than atop a hill. Amongst the Aaru-padai veedu Tiruchendur holds second place after Palani. When Murugan set out to destroy the asura, he destroyed Tarakasuran in the north in a place called Cambay which is between the two rivers Sabarmati and Mahe. He is supposed to have erected a sthamba (pillar) of victory there before proceeding to the South to meet Surapadman.

On the way, Murugan, along with his nine brothers and celestial warriors camped at Tiruchendur. Murugan, on reaching Tiruchendur, sat on a throne in the temple built by Devadakshan. He also sent Veerabahu as a messenger to Surapadman. But in his arrogance and ignorance Surapadman only insulted Veerabahu and threw him in jail. But Veerabahu, who fought a valiant battle, destroyed Attani mandapam and came back to Tiruchendur to report the events to his brother.

Murugan then set out to take on Surapadman face-to-face and a battle ensued that lasted for six days. The battle is described as *Surasamharam* and is celebrated every year at Tiruchendur (city of victory) as Kanda Shashti during the October— November months. Murugan also wanted to build a temple here for his father (Lord Shiva), and the temple was built with the help of the celestial architect, Mayan. Even now the sanctum sanctorum has an image of Murugan worshipping Shiva.

Apart from the Puranic legends the temple also has recorded miracles in recent history. During the 17th century a group of Dutch pirates stole the main idol made from five metals/alloys (panchaloha) but when they set sail their ship was struck by lightning and thunder. Terrified, and knowing the idol was the reason for the powerful storm, they tied it with a rope and dropped it into the ocean. Immediately the storm abated and the pirates set sail.

The people of Tiruchendur were worried when they found the idol of their deity missing but Murugan (who has his own way of showering love on devotees) appeared in the dream of Vadamalayiappa Pillai, an ardent devotee. He showed him the exact place where the idol lay and the devotees found the idol and restored it back to its rightful place.

On the 29th, a Friday in the month of Thai (January), in the Kollam year of 1653 A.D., both Pillai and Nadan (with the help of a few Parthavar fishermen), took a boat to the spot. They were surprised to find a lemon floating at the exact location and Garuda the divine eagle was flying overhead was circling the spot as well. The fishermen dived and retrieved the idol.

This miracle is just one example of the powers and blessings Lord Murugan has showered on his devotees and even has an inscription at the temple. Just like his name Aarumughan, he has faces in all directions and keeps a watch on all the events in this universe. It does not matter to him how big or small the

54

miracle is, when his devotees are in trouble he always appears either directly or indirectly.

This story teaches that everyone should learn to respect other's religions as we respect ours. For the pirates the idol was just something that they could sell to make money. For the entire town that believed in the powers of the Lord, the idol symbolised his very presence.

The temple has many more miracles; it was here that Sri Aadi Shankaracharya was cured of his skin disease after applying the sacred ash and sandal paste. He composed the Shanmukha Bhujangam thereafter which is still recited by devotees to find a cure for many skin (and other) ailments.

To this day, miracles take place every day at the temple. One recorded miracle, for example, is of Desikamurthy Swami, who lived 300 years ago. While he was engaged in the construction of the Mela Gopuram of the temple he found he did not have sufficient funds to pay those that had worked so diligently for him. Accordingly, Swami gave the workers a packet of vibhuthi (sacred ash) at the end of their work day. Once the workers crossed the Thoondu Kai Vinayakar shrine (as instructed by the Swami) the packet of sacred ash turned into the exact amount of wages that each worker was to be paid.

The temple also has a tank called 'Nazhi Kinnaru' which was created by Murugan's vel. When Murugan's army was returning after the battle they felt extremely thirsty. To quench that thirst Murugan hurled his Shakti vel forth and water sprang out of the ground. Today the tank still stands at the same spot. The outer tank which is fourteen square-feet is filled with brackish green water but inside the tank there is a small well which has crystal clear water. This is the spot where the vel landed. Even today people climb down the thirty four steps of the outer tank to reach the miraculous 'Nazhi Kinnaru' with clear water.

Tiruchendur Miracle — Pakalli Koottar

The Saivaites are worshipers of Shiva (and Murugan, being Shiva's son, is part of the Saivaites pantheon) and Vaishnavas stick to worshipping Vishnu and his *avatars* (*avatar* is the highest form of incarnation). But Murugan is so powerful in his beauty and knowledge that he attracts devotees from the Vaishnava sect too. And the most important Vaishnava devotee is Pakalli (aka Pagazhi) Koottar.

Pakalli Koottar was a Vaishnava by birth and lived in a small village called Chaturveda Mangalam nearly a century ago. He was a learned man, but always had excruciating stomach aches. He prayed to different gods but found no relief whatsoever. He prayed to Murugan of Tiruchendur out of desperation and found a miraculous cure.

Koottar then travelled to Tiruchendur to thank Murugan for his mercy. Since he was a poet, he wrote a wonderful piece of work called Pillai Tamil in praise of Murugan. The pundits and scholars at the temple agreed it was one of the finest pieces of literary devotion they had ever seen. Since Pakalli was a Vaishnava, however, they did not bother to honor him.

Nevertheless, since Pakalli was more interested in thanking Murugan than receiving any kind of honor for his work, he went home undisturbed by the events at the temple. But Murugan, who also manifests justice and wisdom, wanted to see his devotee honored and also to teach a lesson to the so-called scholars, a lesson for discrimination based on religious beliefs.

The idol of Murugan in Tiruchendur is adorned with many jewels, so Murugan removed a huge piece of jewel from its chest and transferred it to the chest of Pakalli. The next day the temple authorities were surprised to find the jewel missing and went about searching for it. But when they came upon Pakalli who was adorned with the jewel on his chest they realized the divine play and also their own mistake for dishonoring a true bhakta (devotee) of Murugan. They asked for Pakalli's forgiveness and carried him in a grand procession, around the village in a palanquin proclaiming the miracles of Murugan.

Pakalli's devotional songs are played at the Tiruchendur temple to this day and he holds a prominent place amongst Murugan devotees. This story shows that though we may belong to different sects or religions, when faith is unshakable, divine mercy can be obtained by anyone.

Palani

Palani was the hill top where Lord Murugan settled following defeat by his elder brother, Lord Ganesha. The two had raced around the world to win an apple from their father, Lord Shiva. In anger and defeat, Murugan made his stand for a long time, while Lord Shiva and Devi Parvati and the devatas sang glorious songs in his praise to pacify his anger and bring him back with them to Kailasha. The image of Murugan at Palani is said to be made by a devotee of Lord Skanda known as Bhogar who made it out of the Nava Pashanas (nine herbals/poisons).

The temple is itself situated at a hill station by the same name about twenty miles away from Dindigul Junction situated between Thiruchirapally and Madurai. It is said that this is the only place where devotees of Murugan can approach Him with love and faith because it elevates the minds of the pilgrims.

Rahul Kabade

Palani or Pazham Nee – You are wisdom, so why grieve?

There are so many fascinating aspects to the birth and life of Murugan that there are hundreds of legends associated with him. Perhaps the most enduring one that everyone knows is about his spat with elder brother Ganesha. But just like every other legend this too has many hidden meanings that have to be discovered by a true devotee of Murugan.

The story involves Narada Muni who travels the three worlds and is always found at the center of chaos (though most of his deeds are actually performed to bring order amongst the chaos that he creates). According to legend, when Narada Muni visited Shiva's abode in mount Kailasha, the entire family was present: the two sons Karthikeya, and Ganesha and Shiva's wife Parvati. Narada offers a golden mango to Shiva saying it is the 'jnana pazham' (golden fruit of knowledge) and requests him to eat the fruit. But Shiva seeing his wife Parvati offers it to her. Parvati in turn wants to offer the fruit to her children.

Since the fruit cannot be cut in two, a competition is arranged where the first son to go around the three Universes thrice gets the fruit. Karthikeya (who rides the fast-flying peacock) mounts his vahana (vehicle) and sets off on a tour around the Universe. Ganesha, the big-bellied but wise one, knows he

59

cannot beat his brother on his slow moving vahana, the mouse. So instead he circumambulates his parents thrice. When asked why he did that he answers saying his parents are his Universe. Pleased with Ganesha's love and wisdom, parents Shiva and Parvati give him the golden fruit.

Karthikeya returns from his trip around the Universe only to find his brother already enjoying the fruit. This infuriates him so much that he walks off from Kailasha and settles down on the mountain. Shiva and Parvati come down searching for their son and pacify him saying 'Pazham-Nee' – 'You are the fruit'. Though Karthikeya is pacified, he does not return home with his parents. He stays back on the mountain which later came to be known as Palani (Pazham Nee – 'You are the fruit').

Though the story on this level seems like a simple fight between siblings, the other meanings that can be discerned are many. For instance, one has to overcome ego to attain the 'fruit of knowledge'. Though people believe that the fight between the brothers has not abated to this day, it is not entirely true. In the wooing and marriage of Valli-Murugan, Ganesha plays a very important role. He assumes the form of a terrifying elephant to frighten Valli who, otherwise very brave, is scared of elephants.

The fight for the fruit of knowledge is not the only time that Murugan appears human-like, even if his wisdom is beyond compare. The story is to make devotees understand that wisdom as shown by Lord Ganesha lies in everyday life. Mother and Father are the first true Vedas the other two being Guru and God.

The temple built at Palani is for the worship of Murugan in the form of Dandayudhapani ('the one holding the staff'). Here Murugan has renounced the world and is in his *jnani* stage.

In the present age of Kali Yuga, Murugan plays a very important role so He is also known as Kali Yuga *Vardhan*. The great sages of ancient times were foresighted enough to know that people in Kali Yuga will never have enough time or the patience to undergo the rigorous penance required to experience divine grace. That is the reason why things were simplified so that just chanting the name of Kali Yuga Vardhan Murugan would be enough to start the journey of enlightenment.

Palani — Idumban and Kavadi

Amongst the many festivals celebrated in South India, the Thaipusam festival has an elaborate preparation. It is celebrated on the full moon day during the month of 'Thai' (January—February), but devotees start the preparation forty-eight days in advance. A strict purification ritual is followed to help them purge themselves of all physical and mental impurities.

The 'Kavadi' that is carried during the festival consists of two pieces of semi-circular steel or wood which is bent in the middle and attached to a cross-like structure. This is then balanced on the shoulders of the devotee. Flowers and peacock feathers are used to decorate the Kavadi.

Carrying the Kavadi is not a simple process; it symbolizes transcendence of desire. The devotee actually gives up worldly pleasures like physical relationships and alcohol, and follows a strict regimen of sleeping on the floor, eating a vegetarian diet and bathing in cold water. Such practices make them spiritually fit to carry the Kavadi for Murugan.

The origin of Kavadi and its significance to Murugan is steeped in mythology and is a fascinating account for devotees to understand one more aspect of Murugan's character. Lord Shiva had entrusted two hillocks to the saint Agastya.

Agastya (aka Agastiyar), a dwarf sage had, according to legend, visited Podiyamalai in the south of India at the command of Lord Shiva, to maintain the equilibrium of the earth during Lord Shiva and goddess Parvati's marriage. Most of the prominent gods (and many sages) gathered at Kailasha mountain during the wedding. Hence, to maintain a balance of good forces and divine power in the south, Agastya was asked by Lord Shiva to stay in the south during this wedding. Such is the glory of Agastya!

The two hills entrusted by Shiva were called Shivagiri and Shaktigiri and Agastya wanted them to be installed in the South where he lived. After the epic battle between devatas and asuras Idumban (an asura) repented for his actions and prayed to Murugan for a pardon. He was granted this pardon so he then became a disciple of Agastya. The Sage Agastya, himself, was a great Murugan devotee and it is believed that Murugan taught the Tamil language to the sage when he moved from the north to south of India.

When Agastya wanted the two hillocks moved he asked Idumban to carry it for him to which Idumban readily agreed. He carried the two hillocks slung on his shoulders, like a Kavadi. When he reached Palani he was too tired to continue the journey so he placed the two hills and rested awhile. After some time when Idumban wanted to continue his journey he could not lift the hill and found a small boy wearing just a 'kaupeenam' (loin-cloth) sitting on top of the hill. Idumban asked the boy to vacate the place so he could carry the hill.

The boy of course was Murugan who had arrived in Palani after losing the 'fruit of knowledge' to his brother Ganesha. Murugan was in a rebellious mood when he reached a place called Tiru Avinakudi. When Idumban found the boy on top of the hill, he did not realize it was his ishta devata (favorite god) Murugan. And hence, a fierce battle ensued. Idumban was slain. But as always, Murugan restored Idumban back to life.

Once Idumban realized it was his beloved Murugan, he prayed to Murugan and requested that whoever carries a 'Kavadi' to the temple of Palani should be blessed by the Lord. Idumban also has the privilege of standing sentinel at the hill. Accordingly, to this day devotees going to the Palani temple carry a Kavadi on their shoulders and pay their obeisance to Idumban first since his temple is situated half-way up the Palani hill.

This story shows that Murugan rewards sincere devotion and he embodies the inner-light and grace needed to transform a person no matter what their past may have been. His sincere devotees not only become a part of Him but they also become a part of his legends.

Festival Agni Nakshatram at Palani

Festivals were devised by people over time to commemorate some important event that took place in different eras. Since most of them have a spiritual message, festivals are a way of remembering the past and infusing it with the present so the meaning and importance of the event is not lost to the general population.

The temples built during the Vedic period exist not just to house the presiding deity; they were also built for people to experience the advantages of nature which may not have been present everywhere. For example, building a temple on top of a hill and having festivals surrounding the deity ensured that devotees undertook pilgrimages at least once a year to enjoy nature's bounty and seek divine grace.

Murugan, who is known for his inner and outer manifestation of beauty, youth, wisdom and valor, is also known as the god of mountains, since most of his temples are located atop a mountain. The most important temple amongst all Murugan temples is the Palani temple, because its main idol is built from nine medicinal herbs, unlike granite which is the normal building material, but the festivals are equally esoteric in nature.

The Agni Nakashatram festival at Palani is dedicated to Murugan and it falls during the hottest month of the year (between the 7th through 20th of May). As part of the celebrations, devotees perform an important ritual called the "Girivallam" which is circumambulating the mountain of Palani. The ritual is done during the early morning and according to the legends of Palani it is an act of penance to worship the hill either from afar, near, or by going around it.

People also carry Kavadi here with two pots of water from the river Cauvery and this water is then used to perform the abhishekam (bathing ritual) of the idol. This water is considered the most sacred water by Murugan devotees and is collected as teertham (holy water). People believe drinking the water cures many diseases and some even take it home to perform a ritual cleansing of their homes. The Kavadi is carried in scorching heat, but the devotees of Murugan seem to be oblivious to this and love performing this ritual at the peak of summer every year.

The festival of Agni Nakashatram and the act of girivallam has both spiritual and scientific reasons and it is an ancient practice that has continued over the centuries. The meaning of 'Giri' in Tamil is mountain and 'vallam' means circumambulation. The reason why it is done is not only because it provides devotees peace of mind, but inhaling the fragrances of the hundreds of medicinal herbs that grow on the mountain actually cures many diseases and ensures good health. While circumambulating, one also gets blessed by the various invisible and evolved souls who visit and reside on the hill top. The Kadambam flowers which grow aplenty on the mountains are a Murugan favorite and women devotees adorn their hair with them while doing the girivallam.

During the Agni Nakashatram festival it is also believed that various siddhas (great sages) who live in the caves surrounding the mountain also come out to pay homage to Murugan. Encountering a siddha during such a time is considered the epitome of spiritual experience.

There are few norms that need to be observed while performing the girivallam; the most important one is to fast for the day (so people normally eat only after completing the ritual). The girivallam (or walking around the holy hill) itself is considered a 'walking meditation' so concentrating on the image of Murugan and reciting Om Sharavana Bhava, his main *mantra* increases the divine benefits. But the most surprising part of girivallam at Palani is people can be found chanting 'Jesus Jesus' or even Buddham Sharanam Gachaami because the festival of Agni Nakashatram and the girivallam attracts devotees from every religion.

Another strange, yet spiritual aspect of performing girivallam is to experience the confluence of people from all over the world walking around the mountain as one. It is believed that at a particular time the groups of people performing the girivallam share a karmic connection.

Murugan has been worshipped during all the Yugas known to mankind but he still performs his miracles to this day in ordinary people's lives. To seek Murugan's blessings you don't need to be a great poet or sage. Just chanting his name and going around his abode is enough to receive *moksha* (freedom from the cycle of birth and death) in Kali Yuga.

Siddha Bhogar — Nava Pashanam idol at

Palani

The ancient wisdom of India is so advanced that when people study it today they are amazed by the many advances that were made which now form the basis of science. Amongst the thousands of sages or siddhas, Bhogar, who lived more than 3000 years ago, has a life history that is unparalleled.

The achievements and life of Bhogar are well documented in 'Saptakanda' (an ancient work written by Bhogar's disciple Pulippani). Bhogar's guru Kalanginathar was a mystical sage himself and a great alchemist who passed his knowledge on to Bhogar.

Bhogar who was born in a family of goldsmiths was also well versed in siddha (herbal or ayurvedic) medicine. He practiced Kundalini Yoga in four stages and the Palani malai (mountain) became his center of penance. He is reported to have visited countries like China and South America both in astral and physical forms. It is also believed that when his guru Kalanginathar wanted to attain '*Samadhi*' (last meditative state for a mortal) in China he telepathically called his disciple Bhogar from Tamil Nadu. Bhogar then travelled to China by sea following the trade route. In China he learned more about yoga, siddha and Kaya Kalpa, the herbal formulae to prolong life.

After his guru went into *Samadhi*, Bhogar continued his mission under the name of 'Bo-Yang' which also means 'bliss' (both material and spiritual). He is supposed to have lived in China for many years before returning to Palani in India along with his disciple Yu whom he named Pulippani. On the way they visited Kaurapa, a tantric temple, in Assam. Bhogar composed his work 'Bhogar Sapta Kandam' at Mount Kailasha after seeking the blessings of Lord Shiva. The manuscript originally contained 700,000 verses which he later abridged to 7,000.

On his return to Palani before the beginning of Kali Yuga, (3102 BC) Bhogar met with other siddhas to find the best path for humanity to continue on its spiritual path during the dark age of Kali. Bhakti Yoga (the yoga of love and devotion) was decided as the best path.

Bhogar who was a great Murugan devotee was entrusted with the task of creating an icon that would last the entire Kali Yuga. So Bhogar siddha who was known for many achievements in his oceanic life used 4448 rare herbs and fashioned the nava pashanam. He made the statute of Murugan from this material and installed it at the Palani temple.

Ancient texts reveal that the nine minerals used by Bhogar were Pooram, Veeram, Rasam, Kandagam, Jathilingam, Gauri Pasanam, Vellai Pasanam, Mridharsingh, and Silasat. But nobody can re-create the amalgam to this day. Bhogar believed that by making an abhishekam of milk and panchamritham (a sweet offering made from banana, cardamom, sugar, dates and honey) on the idol, the medicine can be distributed to a whole range of people to cure different diseases.

Holding true to this belief, even today many people eat the 'prasadam' (offerings of food to a deity) of Palani Andavar for relief from all kinds of diseases, especially skin disease. One of the ancient practices at the temple that continues to this day is to apply sandalwood paste overnight on the idol. The next day this paste is removed from the 'moolavar' (idol) and distributed to the devotees. This paste acts as a wonder drug to cure many skin diseases.

The idol is a unique statute and when modern-day scientists tried to test a tiny part of it, they were surprised to find that the material sublimated on heating. This shows that the advancement of science depends on ancient wisdom even to this day. It also shows that Lord Murugan ensures that his devotees have access to him even in the material form. The concept of creating an idol of god itself is unique because it is one way of 'seeing the unseen'. Since god cannot be seen through the human eye, ancient siddhas like Bhogar came up with the idea of creating idols so ordinary people can experience god through a material (object) before moving on to the more complicated part of mental worship. Murugan at Palani has ensured exactly that through his devotee Bhogar.

Bhogar's devotees believe that his *'Swarna Samadhi'* (final resting place, swarna means golden and *samadhi* is the final and highest Yogic stage of union with the Supreme) was built by Bhogar himself right below the foot of the Palani Andavar statute in Palani. Even if he has left the physical plane he is believed to guide his devotees from the astral plane.

Palani visit of Pamban Swami

Pamban Swami (1848 – May 30, 1929) and Lord Murugan are inseparable because the Swamigal lived his whole life dedicated to the service of Murugan, though he was a 'grihastha' (householder). He practiced intense worship (sadhana) and wrote hymns, poems and books praising Lord Murugan and his miracles.

In the year 1848, a boy was born in Pamban Island (which was then a part of the Madras Presidency) and a psychic predicted the boy would grow up to be very famous one day for his words and wisdom. He was named Appavu and had a normal education till the age of thirteen. However when he turned thirteen he had a vision of Murugan in his dream and from then on started composing verses in praise of Murugan. He wrote for a hundred days and each of the verses ended with his manasika (of the mind) guru's name—Arunagirinathar (a different poet and ardent Murugan devotee).

When the temple priest of Pamban, Sri Seddu Madhava Iyer, saw these verses he was very impressed with the language and Appavu's faith in Murugan. He arranged for 'upadesam' (Vedic learning) and also taught Appavu the Sanskrit language. But Appavu's parents did not want him to lead the life of a *sanyasi* (renunciate) so they arranged for his marriage with a girl named Kalimuthami in the year 1878. The couple had two daughters and a son however Appavu still lived like a saint and when his father passed away he took over the family's legal business and won many cases.

Divine miracles kept happening in his life. One night his daughter was crying continuously and though his wife requested Appavau to give vibhuthi (sacred ash) to the child he refused and requested his wife to pray to Murugan and he started to meditate as well. The wife did as she was told and after some time the child stopped crying and was fast asleep. Appavu was surprised and asked his wife what had happened. She told him that when he was in his trance an old saint came to the house and applied vibhuthi on the child's forehead and went away immediately. Appavu knew it was his Murugan.

Since he would leave his family back at Pamban Island in search of Murugan, Appavu soon came to be called Pamban Swami or Pamban Swamigal. But miracles never stopped in his life. His wife was always afraid he would leave home and one day when Pamban Swami announced he was going to Palani, she feared he would never come back and she asked a friend to stop him from taking the journey. The friend, who did not want to offend him, asked if he had Murugan's permission to visit Palani. Pamban Swami who was desperate to see Murugan at Palani said 'yes' and went up to the terrace to mediate. No sooner had he sat down — he heard a voice saying: 'Did I ask you to come to Palani?' Pamban Swami knew it was Murugan speaking so he answered 'no' and the voice then said that Swami should not go to Palani unless called.

Unfortunately the call never came and Pamban Swami never visited Palani though he begged Murugan in all his poems to call him to Palani. But that did not stop him from writing praises of Murugan. He wrote the Shanmukha Kavacham (1891) which is a powerful hymn with thirty verses. It is still recited by devotees today in Palani and in fact in all Murugan temples. The poem asks for Murugan's protection from bodily and mental illness. He also asks for protection from enemies, wild beasts, demons, devils, poisonous creatures and insects. Devotees who have recited the Kavacham have experienced miraculous cures for various diseases.

Pamban Swami also wrote the 'Panchamritham Varnam' and Murugan has said to an old lady in Tiruchendur that he will be physically present wherever the poem was sung and set to a pleasant note. Devotees still believe that singing the Panchamritham Varnam is equal to performing abhishekam and pooja to the Lord.

Pamban Swami during his lifetime has written 6,666 poems, 1000 names of Lord Murugan and thirty two viyasams. It is believed that reciting his Gnanamurtham benefits devotees both in this life and in the afterlife. Swami went into *Samadhi* on 30th May 1929 and his *Samadhi* at Tiruvanmiyur, Chennai is still visited by scores of Murugan devotees.

This story shows how Lord Murugan helped Pamban Swami, who in turn helped thousands of other devotees through his work.

Swami Malai

Swami Malai (meaning 'Gods mountain') is the name of a hill situated close to the Kumbakonam town in South India. It is approximately 200 miles out of Chennai along the Chennai— Thiruchirapally main line. Swamimalai is situated on the banks of a tributary of river Cauvery.

The mythology of this temple is also related to Sage Bhrigu. Sage Bhrigu had a boon that anybody who disturbs his penance or meditation will forget all his knowledge. Long ago, Sage Bhrigu once performed intense penance such that the sacred fire emanating from his head reached heavens, and frightened devatas and Indra.

The devatas surrendered to Lord Shiva praying for his grace and relief. Shiva extinguished the sacred fire by covering Sage Bhrigu's head with his hand. As Sage Bhrigu's penance was disturbed his boon came into effect and Shiva became oblivious of his knowledge. It is said that Lord Shiva regained this by learning the *Pranava mantra* from Murugan at this shrine.

As mentioned previously, after Murugan imprisoned Brahma, Shiva summoned Murugan asking his son for Brahma's subsequent release. After the release of Brahma, Shiva requested that he be taught the secret of the *Pranava Mantra*, to which Murugan agreed, on the one condition that his father behave as a disciple and he be respected as his guru. Hence, this place is sacred because it is the guru's shrine where the father Lord Shiva became the pupil, while the son Lord Murugan is depicted as the teacher.

Pazhamudircholai

Pazhamudircholai is the sixth battle camp of Murugan and is situated some sixteen miles out of Madurai atop a densely-forested hill, rich in many fruit trees. This forest is a place where Devi Valli is said to have lived her life.

There is little consensus among scholars on the location of this temple and many local temples are also credited with an equal merit. While the place has ancient origin, the temple was constructed recently. The 'Vel' has been worshipped as the presiding deity for a long time.

It is also said to be the place where Murugan, through the grace of his presence, imparted divine wisdom to the Great Tamilian poet, Avvayar after putting her through a test.

Avvayar at Pazhamudircholai

Avvayar is a well-known Tamil poetess. Her knowledge in Tamil is vast. She is also one of the great devotees of Lord Murugan. One day she went through an incident that made her realize that learning never ends.

As the story goes, she went on a pilgrimage. During this pilgrimage she went to all of the temples on her way (and she was traveling quite a long way). Once, during her pilgrimage, she became very tried and thirsty. Thankfully, she came across a fruit tree and decided to relax under the shadow of this tree and so sat down.

While she was relaxing, she looked up and saw that the tree indeed bore much fruit. The fragrance of the ripe fruit came to entreat her to pick some of the fruit to eat them, but to no avail. She had traveled a long way and was weak. At the same time there was a little boy sitting on one of the branches of the tree. He was also eating fruits. The boy looked down where Avvayar was sitting and thought she looked tired. Looking at the Poetess Avvayar, the boy asked if she wanted some fruit. Avvayar immediately said, "Yes, I'm hungry and thirsty and would like some fruit".

The boy said he would pick some fruits for Poetess Avvayar and asked if she wanted roasted fruits or un-roasted fruits. Avvayar was surprised by the child's question. She wondered in what world could there be both roasted and un-roasted fruits on a tree. She even thought, perhaps, that the village boy did not have any basic knowledge of the language, and thinking so, felt pity for the little boy.

Being tired, however, she had no energy to argue with a small boy, and anyway figured it to be pointless. So ... overlooking everything ... she said to that child that she wanted roasted fruits.

The little boy began his work. Soon enough the boy plucked an over-abundance of fruit which he dropped to the ground and, largely, it fell into mud. Avvayar picked the fruit from the mud and of course had no water with which to wash the fruit. So, to remove the mud, Avvayar had no choice but to try and blow the fruits to clean them. The small boy laughed, looking at Avvayar, and so she asked the boy why he was laughing.

The little boy asked Poetess Avvayar, if the fruits were still hot, because she blew at the fruits as if to cool them down.

Avvayar was surprised by the cleverness of the boy and knew that he had gotten the better of her. As she wondered how a village boy could have so much knowledge and wisdom, she was astonished and looked up, seeing that the boy had a smile on his face.

Surprised, Poetess Avvayar asked him, "Who are you"? Again the boy laughed. He asked Poetess Avvayar, if she couldn't recognize Him. Avvayar suddenly realized who it was, saying, it can be none other than Lord Murugan.

Immediately the small boy disappeared. Lord Murugan appeared in front of Poetess Avvayar. Avvayar realized that it was a leela (a divine act, play or performance designed to impress) of Lord Murugan. He told Avvayar that, "You thought that you had learned everything, but I wanted to show you that learning never ends". Avvayar realized her fault. She understood that Lord Murugan came as a small boy to teach her this very lesson. Realizing her fault, she apologized to Lord Murugan. The place in which this drama happened is known as Pazhamudircholai. It is one of the six abodes of Lord Murugan.

Avvayar thought that a small boy could not beat her in her knowledge of Tamil. But Lord Murugan came, played a drama with fruits, and showed her that knowledge is vast and unending.

Learning is unending—it ends only when all learning is transformed into unconditional love.

Tiruttani

This temple is situated on a hill at Tiruttani in Tamil Nadu and it has 365 steps leading up to the temple in accordance with the total number of days in a year.

There are many legends associated with this temple for Lord Murugan and one of them says that after Lord Indra gave his daughter in the hand of marriage to Murugan, he also gifted him as dowry his most precious possession, his own elephant by the name of Airavatam. Lord Indra's wealth and prosperity started to slump after separating himself from his elephant; upon discovery of which, Murugan suggested he return the elephant. Bound by protocol, Indra refused but requested that the elephant always face in his direction. That is why the elephant idols at Murugan temples everywhere face the direction of east towards Lord Indra. It is said that this event occurred at Tiruttani.

Tiruttani Murugan Worship

Like many Vedic temples in India the Tiruttani temple of Murugan also has its beginnings in the Puranas. Since it is amongst the six battle houses of Murugan, its origin can be traced back to Skanda Purana.

Tiruttani is also known as the 'Shanthipuri' (Abode of Peace) because after the *Surasamharam*, the battle involving Murugan and the asura Surapadman, Murugan found peace and tranquility at this place. After quelling the asuras, the anger and indignation of the Murugan met calm here, and the place continues to offer mental solace to devotees from different Yugas to this day.

The temple has four important teerthams (sacred waters) 'Brahma teertham', Naga teertham', 'Vishnu teertham' and 'Sharavana Poigai', which have offered strength and power to all who worshipped here. In the Treta Yuga, Lord Rama came to Tiruttani after his battle with Ravana and prayed to Lord Murugan (or Thanikesan as he is known here). Sri Rama also found mental peace here after his long battle.

In the Dwapara Yuga, Arjuna came to Tiruttani on his way to teertha yatra (pilgrimage or sacred journey). He prayed to Lord Murugan for power and strength and took a sacred dip in the teertham. During the asuras' reign of terror over the devatas, Tarakasuran, brother of Surapadman, had seized the 'Chakra' (sacred wheel) and 'Shankha' (sacred conch) of Lord Vishnu. It was after offering prayers at Tiruttani that Lord Vishnu got back both his powerful weapons.

I have already narrated the imprisonment of Brahma by Murugan. After Brahma offered his prayers at a spring called 'Brahmasonai' here in Tiruttani, the creation function of the world was restored to him.

The King of serpents, Vasuki, acquired many wounds on his body because he was used as a rope during the churning of the 'amruta' (nectar of immortality) during 'samudra manthan'. All his wounds were healed after praying to Murugan (or Thanikesan) at Tiruttani. The great Sage Agastya worshipped Murugan here and legend has it that Murugan Himself taught the Tamil language to Agastya, since he was from Northern India and knew only Sanskrit.

The Tiruttani temple and its holy teerthams also have historical and literary references. Arunagirinathar the great Tamil poet who lived around 600 years ago has written about Tiruttani. He compares the place to Shivaloka and the soul of the world. Nanda Devi also worshipped Murugan here on the banks of the Nandi River and learned all about the unique relationship a *Jivatma* and *Paramatma* enjoy.

The miracles of Murugan have not abated; Sri Muttuswami Deekshitar who is today considered one of the trinity of

Carnatic music had his inspiration at Tiruttani. Deekshitar who lived nearly 200 years ago also had the fortune of meeting Murugan in the form of an old man on the steps of the temple. Murugan offered *prasadam* from the temple to Deekshitar. This impelled him to compose his first song in praise of Murugan called 'Sri Nathadhi Guruguho Jayathi Jayathi'.

Saint Ramalinga Swamigal, another ardent devotee of Murugan, was blessed with His vision in a mirror in his puja room. Swamigal who lived around 150 years ago was then invited to come to Tiruttani by Murugan after which, Swamigal composed and sang the 'arupta' (miracle) songs of Murugan in chaste Tamil.

The miracles and grace of Murugan as Thanikesan continues at Tiruttani today and it is not a rare sight to find people from Australia, Europe and the US taking a dip at the Sharavana Poigai. The teertham has many minerals (like sulfur and iron), and a bath in the tank refreshes the body and mind.

The Aadi Karthigai festival at Tiruttani (July—August) draws millions of devotees from all over the world who come to offer their prayers and find peace at the feet of Murugan. They bring in 'kavadis' and 'pal kodum' (milk pot) to give their thanks and chant 'Muruganukku Aaro Hara' in total ecstasy.

Indrasonai of Tiruttani

The Puranas are filled with mythological stories and legends that sometimes defy logic but they were written and handed down through generations to help mankind. Their very purpose was to show the path of enlightenment and since not all are ready to perform austere penance, the stories in the Puranas offer us an easy way to understand the deeper meaning of life.

The *Surasamharam* of Murugan is a well-documented account of how Murugan destroyed the army of asuras (demons) led by Surapadman. Since the battle was fought across many places there are more than a few important places on earth, where Murugan made his presence felt during and after the battle. These important sthalas (places) also became mukti (liberation) sthalas. But since the sanctity of the sthala took place during the epic battle they also came to be called Padai veedu (battle houses).

All of the temples have their origin in Skanda Purana though newer buildings have been added, destroyed, and rebuilt again over the ages. These six battle houses are mentioned in various works like Thirumurugatupadai (a body of work by saint and poet Nakkirar). They are mentioned in Sangam Kaalam (3rd century B.C. to 4th century A.D.) literature like Tholkapiyam and Arunagirinathar's various works on Murugan.

Each house has its own legend and the Tiruttani temple where Murugan found peace after the battle has many legends to its credit. I have covered the marriage of Murugan to Deviyani earlier where Indra gave the celestial elephant Airavatam and why that elephant always faces eastwards.

Another legend connected to Indra and Murugan also contains an interesting story. During the terror reign of the asuras' the wealth of Devaloka was either destroyed or looted. It is believed an asura called Titan had seized precious wealth like the Padmaneeti, Sanghaneeti and Chintamani from Devaloka. In order to get them back from the asura, Indra prayed at Tiruttani to Murugan.

It is said that Indra planted a rare plant called Karunkuvalai in the pool known as Indrasonai. This rare and beautiful plant offered only three flowers a day. Indra used these flowers to worship Lord Murugan thrice a day to get back his wealth. And just like in all Murugan legends, Murugan blessed and restored the precious wealth of Indra to him.

Though the ultimate goal of any Murugan devotee is to be 'one with god', Murugan also looks after the worldly affairs of the bhakta. Even worldly pleasures like wealth, health, and education can be prayed for without hesitation.

The story of Indra and the Indrasonai pond says that we can pray to Murugan even to this day for wealth and happiness.

The Indrasonai or Indra teertham still exists in Tiruttani and people bathe here to gain prosperity and wealth.

We do not have to perform austere penance like the sages do in order to reach Him. By following simple rituals and singing hymns Murugan offers both worldly and spiritual wealth to his devotees.

OTHER MURUGAN TEMPLES OF PROMINENCE

Although the previously detailed accounts of the six temples are given utmost importance in Sangam literature, there are many other temples spread across India and the world that deserve some mention not only for their legends but also for their spiritual significance.

Marudamalai

Considered the next most important temple after the Aarupadai Veedu temples, it is situated at Coimbatore in Tamil Nadu and is associated with the Paambatti siddha—the snake charming sage of South India—who is said to have been a staunch devotee of Lord Murugan. It was on the hills of Marudamalai that devatas had awaited the advent of Murugan on the advice of Lord Shiva to seek protection from Surapadman. It is also believed that the divine cow Kamadhenu has grazed on the hills where the temple is located.

Vayalur

Situated roughly nine kilometers from Trichy in Tamil Nadu, it is well connected via rail lines to the rest of India. The legend surrounding this Murugan temple is that a Sage by the name of Arunagirinathar was blessed at this spot. The temple is also known for its Shakti Teertha bathing tank and it is common belief that Lord Murugan Himself created this tank with his spear.

Ettukudi

The temple is associated with a simple story surrounding a sculpture that was the envy of one of the Chola rulers who cut off his thumb in protest. He shifted base to a location today called Ettukudi where he made another sculpture of Murugan with equal brilliance, surviving through the pain only because Murugan graced him with His presence. The sculpture here of Lord Murugan has three faces and twelve arms seated on a north facing peacock with the entire weight of the sculpture resting on peacock legs.

Viralimalai

Located some seventeen miles from Trichy, the Viralimalai temple is just as famous as the most prominent of Murugan temples. It is said that this temple is where many sages and hermits offered prayers to Murugan in the form of Kura trees. The temple is in the heart of the town Viralimalai and hence the name Viralimalai. The temple is specially known for the many peacocks found on the rocky hill as well as the unique offering of a cigar to Murugan as Dandayudhapani.

Viralimalai Murugan and Sage Vashistha

To find out about the various Murugan leelas during different periods a study of literature starting from the Sangam Kaalam provides many accounts. One such documented deed is how the Viralimalai Murugan temple came into being and the many events surrounding it.

This temple of Murugan is built on top of a hill and the 'sthala puranam' of the temple explains that saints and sages live around the mountain in the form of *Kura* trees. The greatest Murugan devotee poet and saint, Arunagirinathar, explains in his songs about this phenomenon. It was for this reason the place was called Viravi Malai and later got to be known as Viralimalai. Viravi in Tamil means 'spread', and here it is the Kura trees which are spread about the hill.

Arunagirinathar himself visited this place after being directed to do so in a dream. According to the account the poet lost his way inside the forest surrounding the hill. Out of nowhere a 'Veddan' (hunter) came in and gave the poet directions to reach the hill and then disappeared without a trace. It was only later that Arunagirinathar realized that the hunter was none other than his beloved Murugan. He explains this with a song in his work 'Thiruppugazh'.

Another legend about the hill and Lord Murugan's benevolence involves a Palayakamrar (a tribe) representative called Karupumuthu Pillai. According to this legend Pillai used to visit the Viralimalai shrine every Friday and offered his prayers. But once, during his weekly visit, the river Mamundi was flooded after the bunds were broken due to heavy rains. Pillai was left stranded, cut off from the mainland.

With no food or water Pillai (a chain smoker) was miserable but Lord Murugan appeared before him and offered him a cigar. He even took Pillai to the temple for a darshan. After this incident the cigar became part of naivedyam (or sacred food) offered to Lord Murugan in this temple. This only proves that nobody can understand the mysterious ways of Murugan.

The Sthala Puranam of Viralimalai also has a mythological account involving Sage Vashistha, a *Saptarishi*, and his wife Arundhati who was the daughter of the first yoga teacher, Patanjali. It is said that Arundhati once neglected her duty of feeding Lord Murugan. This angered her husband so much that he cursed her, but Murugan, who is always behind his devotees, in turn cursed the sage. Both husband and wife later came to Viralimalai and prayed to Lord Murugan and had their curses reversed. Many a time other saints and sages who were cursed for various reasons have also landed here (including the sages Kashyapa and Narada). They each prayed at this place to ward off their respective curses.

Lord Murugan appears in Viralimalai in his 'Aarumughan' aspect seated on his peacock, flanked by his divine consorts

Valli and Deviyani. The significance of the temple is that Murugan here blesses the 'indriyas' or senses of his devotees.

Kataragama or Kadirkama and Nallur

These two temples dedicated to the worship of Murugan are situated on the plains of Sri Lanka. They are believed to date back very far into history and have equally-alluring legends associated with them. The Kadirkaaman temple is not just a holy place for Hindus but also for Buddhists as well. Nallur, however, is completely dedicated to the worship of Murugan and Hindus alone.

Story of Kataragama– Dakshin Kailasha

Kataragama is best known as the Dakshin Kailasha (southern abode of Lord Shiva) and ironically it lies in the same longitude —80.10 as the Kailasha in the Himalayas. It is also known as the abode of Kumaran (the Tamil god of beauty and eternal youth). Kataragama has its own unique story that is as fascinating as any of the other Kumaran legends. But it also has historical reference because the place is mentioned in the Skanda Purana as well.

The story of Kataragama begins with Murugan incarnating as Kataragama and living in Tamil Nadu along with his spouse Deviyani which is in fact the distorted name of Devasena. One day Kataragama and Deviyani have a huge quarrel and Kataragama walks away to the island of Sri Lanka in anger.

He lives and hunts in the hills where he meets the adopted daughter of the tribal hunter (Veddan) named Valli. The Kataragama—Valli romance is very similar to the Kanda Puranam story where Kataragama tries to woo Valli in different guises instead of his true form. Valli who had already vowed to marry none but Murugan rebukes him as a hunter and an old man. But when Murugan shows her his true form Valli agrees to marry and they live happily for many years amongst the Veddans.

Meanwhile Deviyani who is tired of her single life sends Katargama's guru Muttulingam Swami and a Muslim person called Mohammed Navi to search for Kataragama. They search for him in the hills in vain until finally one day Muttulingam Swami finds that someone has smoked half of his opium pipe and concludes that only Kataragama can do this. They finally locate Kataragama living with the Veddans and try to persuade him to return to Deviyani but he refuses. While Swami stays behind, Mohammed Navi returns to Deviyani and tells her the entire story.

Deviyani immediately sets off to bring back her husband but when she reaches the island she, along with Navi, stays with the Veddans till the end. After their passing away, the

Veddans build a temple for Muttulingam Swami and a Mosque for Mohammed Navi on either side of Valli's temple.

This story has many layers apart from the obvious one of Murugan incarnating and his romance. The fact that He descended from Uttara (north) to Dakshin (south) signifies the descent of the Spirit into matter. The romance between Murugan and Valli is an allegory where the *Paramatma* comes down and woos the *Jivatma* represented by an ordinary hunter girl Valli.

When wooing Valli, Murugan who is already aware of Valli's vow to marry him does not show her his true form at once. He plays with her using different guises. Here Murugan is a playful god who loves to play and test his devotees. But it also holds another esoteric meaning because the true devotee of Murugan is supposed to penetrate all his disguises and experience him in his true, formless nature.

Kataragama also has a beautiful meaning in its very name, the word 'Kadir' or Katir means light or effulgence and 'Kaman' means passion or love. So it also means that the light or *Paramatma* comes down to unite with the love and passion of the *atman* (soul). In Kataragama, Murugan has no idol; He is represented as pure consciousness.

The sanctum sanctorum in Kataragama only has a small casket which holds the shat-kona yantra (the six-faced triangle). Its two triangles, interlocked, represent the six faces of Shanmukha and since the temple is located amongst seven hills it is another dimension in understanding the Supreme. The number seven represents the return and integration of the soul into its original form which is pure innocence. Worshipping Kumaran in his formless aspect helps devotees experience Him in his original aspect.

Kataragama is one of those mystical places on earth which attracts people, not only because of the legends associated with it, but also the very atmosphere is serene and soul-soothing. It is believed that Bhogar an ardent devotee of Murugan visited Kataragama and sought his blessings. His disciple Kalyana Giri (or Babaji as he is popularly known here) is supposed to have taught the different rituals that are performed even today.

It is one place every Murugan devotee visits at least once in a lifetime to evoke Murugan's mercy but strangely enough the place cannot be visited unless Murugan Himself issues an invitation to the devotee.

Sri Kukke Subrahmanya Kshetra—Snake-King

India is dotted with many kshetra (places) that have religious significance rooted in tradition and mythology and dedicated to various deities. Each has their own legend. Kukke Subrahmanya, which is now situated in Dakshin Kannada, the present day Karnataka, has its origins in the Skanda Purana.

Earlier, I have mentioned that the marriage of Deviyani and Murugan took place at Thiruparamkundram. However, there is another version of the marriage having taken place elsewhere. In this version, after the epic battle of the asuras (demons) and devatas (gods) in which Murugan destroyed the asuras, He, along with his brothers Ganesha and Veerabahu, visit a mountain called Kumara parvatha (mountain). Lord Indra received Murugan and his brothers and also requested Murugan to marry his daughter Devasena. The marriage was solemnized at Kumara parvatha and was attended by all celestial beings and water from several holy rivers was bought for the abhishekam. The river Kumaradhara was formed from the waters of this abhisheka.

It is also believed that Murugan washed his 'Shakti Ayudha' (battle axe) in the river Kumaradhara. The present-day temple is built on the banks of this river. Here Subrahmanya also has a very distinctive Kannada name. He is also known as 'Kukke Pattana'.

The 'Sahyadri Khanda' of Skanda Purana has an interesting chapter, Tirthkshetra Mahimnipurana, which gives a brilliant description of the Kukke Subrahmanya kshetra. According to the legend, Garuda (Lord Vishnu's mount eagle) once went on a snake-hunting spree and found Vasuki the serpent-king hiding in the caves of Biladvara, near the present day Kukke Subrahmanya temple. Garuda started to attack Vasuki but, owing to the big size and many jewels (Nagamani) on Vasuki's head, Garuda could not kill him. He also got tired from the poisonous fumes showered by Vasuki.

The great Sage Kashyapa Muni, who is father to both Garuda and Vasuki, requested Garuda to stop trying to kill Vasuki because he was an ardent Shiv-bhakta (being coiled around Lord Shiva's neck). Garuda immediately agrees and spares Vasuki's life.

Kashyapa Muni also advised Vasuki to go to Subrahmanya kshetra and pray to Lord Shiva to get protection from Garuda. Lord Shiva, pleased with Vasuki's devotion and penance, tells the serpent-king that his son will appear in the next 'kalpa' and bless him and that he would then permanently stay there with him. Accordingly, when Murugan went back after the epic battle, He stayed there forever. Murugan also installed a *linga* (idol representation of Lord Shiva, representing the form of the 'formless one') in the form of Bhairava Kapileshavara, a fierce characteristic of his father Lord Shiva, which can still be found to the south of the temple. Murugan installed this linga and Lord Brahma installed the deity of Murugan as Subrahmanya and Vasuki here.

The temple that came to be built at this punya (holy) site became so famous over the years that, apart from the scores of ordinary devotees that visit this place, many prominent sages and pundits have visited Kukke Subrahmanya to receive the blessings of Lord Subrahmanya. The temple also holds six of the eight 'saligrama-silas' which were presented to Madhava (Vishnu) when he visited Badrinath, by Veda Vyasa. In this respect, this place is also very important for Vaisanavas.

Over different Yugas different people have visited this important 'mukti sthala' (place of liberation). Lord Parashurama an incarnation of Lord Vishnu visited the place in Tetra-Yuga to absolve his sins after eliminating the Kshatriya race twenty one times. He is believed to have bathed in the river Kumaradhara and granted forgiveness. Samba, son of Sri Krishna, visited Kukke in the Dwapara Yuga to cure himself of leprosy. Samba smeared the mud from the banks of the river all over his body and was cured of the disease after taking a bath in the river. This custom continues to this day as devotees get cured of all kinds of skin disease after bathing in the river. Pandavas and Aadi Shankaracharya have visited this place and Sri Shankaracharya refers to Kukke as 'Bhaje Kukke Lingam' in his great work, Subrahmanya Bhujangaprayata.

The place has miraculous healing power and Murugan's legacy is a boon to ailing devotees. Every legend of Murugan leaves a boon for his followers for eons. He is as powerful and compassionate (and very much present today) as he has been over all these many years.

Sivan Malai

Temples and their festivals are an important way of uniting people and have been part of the Indian culture since time immemorial. Most temples are built around hills or the tops of mountains so people can benefit from the close interaction with nature while visiting. One is also required to climb to the top as a penance before reaching the door or steps of the temple.

Lord Murugan has scores of temples built in different hills in the South of India but none hold the historical, spiritual and esoteric significance like the Sivan Malai. The literal translation of the name means 'Mountain of Shiva' but the presiding deity, Murugan in another aspect, embodies the power of Shiva, Vishnu, Brahma, Ganesha and Indra.

Though Sivan Malai is not part of the six battlements of Murugan, it is the most powerful and most popular of Murugan temples. The mountain itself has been called by different names in different Yugas. At different times it has been known as Vellimalai, Panamalai, in the age of Kali Yuga it is called the Kamarupa Jothigiri.

The mountain is of interest because during the fight against the demons, Shiva conquers three celestial cities (Tripura) by making a bow out of Mount Meru and the bow-string is Vasuki the King of serpents. After Tarakasuran was vanquished, his sons performed intense penance to please Brahma. Lord Brahma granted them a boon of impregnable and everlasting fortresses that could only be destroyed by one arrow of Lord Shiva. The three mobile cities were designed by Maya in such a manner that they only fall in a straight line on rare occasions which occurs when a heavenly star named Pushya is in conjunction with the Moon; once in a thousand years. The city of iron walls was built on earth, silver walls in the sky and golden walls in heaven. In time, the asura tendencies came back and the cities grew impious and the asuras started troubling the devatas. During the celestial battle, a tip of Shiva's bow, which is mount Meru, falls on earth to become the present day Sivanmalai. Shiva did not require a bow or arrow to destroy these cities; He actually destroyed them without using the chariot the devatas had built. But when Brahma pleaded that the devatas would become a matter of laughter, Shiva, in his infinite grace took up the bow and arrow. The "smile and burn" act of Shiva in Tamil is referred to as "sirithu purameritha peruman", god who laughed and burned the three cities. It is also referred to as Shakti Malai because goddess Parvati did penance here to marry Shiva.

In addition, the mountain has been associated with various sages and saints over the ages. It is believed Sage Agastya performed rigorous penance here to understand the Agamas. The Agamas are the doctrines dealing with philosophical and spiritual know-how in relation to worship of a deity. He is supposed to have carried the water of river Ganga in his Kamandalam (drinking pot) and created a natural water spring out of it.

When Lord Hanuman was on the way to Lanka to meet Devi Sita, consort of Lord Sri Rama, the Sage Vyasa is supposed to have directed him to pray at Sivanmalai. After his penance here Hanuman was blessed with great powers to enable him to fulfill his mission for Lord Sri Rama. Plenty of miracles have taken place in different eras at the mountain. When King Nakutan, for example, was cursed by Agastya and became a snake, he was directed by another Sage, Durvasa, to pray to Sivanmalai Murugan. Needless to say his curse was lifted immediately.

Also, the mountain is surrounded by various teerthas (holy waters) and they are named Agastya, Indra, Brahmananda, Mangala, Veera and Anuma teertham. The waters here have curative properties and are believed to cure many skin diseases. It is believed King Muchukunda was cured of leprosy after he bathed in the Sivanmalai teertham.

Apart from various Murugan devotees the mountain is also the abode of many siddhas who know the value and importance of various herbs that grow around the mountain. 'Jothi pullu' a type of grass that grows there, for example, helps slow down aging process. It is also supposed to glow in the dark.

Arunagirinathar, the great Murugan devotee who composed the 'Thiruppugazh', 'Kandar Alangaram', and 'Kandar Anbuthi' is supposed to have visited Sivanmalai thrice in his lifetime. Praises about the deity and the mountain itself can be found in his work 'Thiruppugazh'.

Though women saints like Karaikkal Ammaiyar, Mangayakarasi, Isaignani, Tilakavathi and Avvayar have sung praises of the Sivan Malai, the mountain also has a woman saint of its own. Valli or 'Amma Sadaichi' as she was popularly known (because her hair grew in long matted locks) was from Sivan Malai. Apart from doing penance standing in front of the sanctum of the temple, she also built wells and resting places for devotees who came from afar to Sivanmalai. She served the pilgrims of Murugan as much as she served Murugan.

She was so 'one' with her Lord Murugan that she pleaded to him saying she will come to Kailasha to meet him. But Murugan, the ever benevolent god, asked Sadaichi to stay at Sivanmalai while he came down to meet her. She is supposed to have disappeared after that but her voice could still be heard in the mountains. So Murugan devotees made a statue of her and placed it at the foot of the altar and sing praises to her to this day.

The Sivan Malai stands today welcoming Murugan bhaktas from all walks of life, as it has done during all eons past. The miracles and faith continue unabated and befitting his name of Kali Yuga Vardhan, Lord Murugan continues to bless his devotees in this age of Kali too.

Batu Caves: Miracles

As far as the miracles of Batu Cave Temple and Englishmen go, it is well-known that when the twentieth century began, the British occupied India. One of the owners of a rubber plantation had taken a few workers from India to a cave to collect droppings of bats. The droppings were collected from the cave and used as manure in the rubber plantation. A spear was apparently found in the very same place in the ground where the present Lord Murugan's idol has been kept.

Lord Murugan's insignia is the spear (vel). The vel is worshipped by Hindu's all over the world. This weapon is synonymous with Murugan and his power to ensure the victory of good over evil. Upon seeing the spear people immediately began to worship it. Incense and flowers were used in the worshipping process. It is but natural that the British had no clue about what was going on and what this worship was all about. They had never witnessed any kind of worship like this before. According to them, these people were a superstitious bunch. The Englishman considered this worship of the vel to be nonsense. He thought that Indians were only wasting their time with such superstitious beliefs.

The Englishman became very angry, started to crack his whip, and asked the Indian workers to continue with their work. According to him, instead of wasting precious time in having this fetish it was better for them to continue working. However the workers did not listen to the Englishman and continued with their worship. This is where the power of devotion came into play.

With anger the Englishman moved forward and from the ground plucked the vel and dumped it into a corner of a dirt heap. The workers were shocked with disbelief and gave a warning to the Englishman that the consequences to follow would be terrible. The Englishman kept laughing and scorning the ignorance of the workers as he felt that he was much more intelligent than the ordinary workers. However, he was on the verge of tasting Murugan's power and might.

Soon after this, the Englishman developed a disease that no one had ever encountered. He fell ill so gravely that his health quickly deteriorated. It was impossible for any doctor to conduct an exact diagnosis of the disease. This time, in his humble and weak mind, he envisioned Lord Murugan. In that vision Murugan told him that if the spear was planted back into its original place, he would get well.

The Englishman became much wiser due to his miseries. So, he went, located the spear and placed it back where it was originally. He did so with a lot of repentance and out of a realisation of the power behind the spear. He also allowed the Tamil workers to continue worshipping the spear. As of now, a temple has been built in the name of Murugan which has prospered and grown. Thousands of devotees and tourists from India and different countries of the world visit Murugan's shrine.

While some come to tour the shrine, the rest are staunch devotees of Lord Murugan. At this shrine many miracles have supposedly taken place. It is said that at the very location of the spear, Mouni Swami had his own powerful presence for many years. He had meditated in this spot for many years in the name of Lord Murugan and achieved many *siddhis* (supernatural powers).

The story is a wonderful example of Lord Murugan teaching visitors that we should respect the culture of others at all times. We should not, at any point in time, judge other cultures by our own standards. Devotees should remember that it is the earnestness of the heart that wins over Murugan and defiling that which is consecrated will only incur wrath. What goes around comes around!

Vetrivel Murugan – Cuddalore

The story of Vetrivel Murugan – Cuddalore is quite intriguing. It embodies the power of Murugan to heal and consecrate the devotees and devotion itself. All that is needed is the faith to receive.

At Cuddalore lived a man with absolutely no belief in God. Once, for many days he was ill and remained bed-ridden. He was administered treatments of different kinds, but nothing seemed to cure him. The doctors had no alternative but to declare that very soon his life would end and this made everyone around him very sad.

At that very time this man had a feeling that Lord Murugan, seated on a peacock, had appeared before him. Instantly he arose from his bed on his own and started calling out to the relatives stating that he was very hungry and needed to eat food urgently. As soon as food was served, he ate, and after that he was cured completely to the surprise of all his relatives.

This man was so humbled with Murugan's *darshan* (sight, glimpse or vision) that in his name he erected a temple. The image of Murugan was sculpted as it was revealed to him. At that very place you get to see the image of Vetrivel Murugan. Also, a particular ritual which involves wiping the idol with betel leaves called "Vetrilai Thudaippu" is followed at the temple.

Those who face difficulties in getting married follow this ritual. Devotees are made to sit near the flag post, while the betel leaf to be offered to the deity is given to them. The holy water is sprinkled on the leaf and with this leaf the devotees wipe their faces and worship Murugan. It is believed that after conducting such a ritual the person is soon married.

In many of the Hindu traditions, the betel leaf is considered very sacred. By using the betel leaf for wiping ones face, the wiping off of all evils also takes place. It is on the basis of this strong faith that the benefits are bestowed on the devotee for which the ritual is performed. Couples who are childless offer lime fruit and three tubers of turmeric to Vetrivel Murugan in worship in their hope for progeny.

As prasadam the very same offerings are returned to the devotee. The lime juice is to be drunk by the couple and the three tubers of turmeric paste needs to be ground and applied on the body by the wife every day. It is believed that the couple will be blessed with children soon after. The coconut also has special significance in the worship of Murugan. Offering the coconut signifies offering our 'ego' as in *ahamkara* or 'head' in an esoteric sense; it is a symbolic gesture of surrender.

In this temple Lord Murugan is seated on a peacock with the right hand raised to bless devotees. He is shown without his spouses, Deviyani and Valli. With pomp and show Vaikaasi Visaakam festival is celebrated. Murugan is taken around the town seated on a swing in a procession at this time. On other important days and festivities such as Panguni Uthiram, Krithigai and Thaipusam, a special abhishekam is done.

The story is a true reflection of what faith can do. When a saint was suffering from disease, Lord Murugan appeared in front of him and made him eat his holy food. He was cured. With faith one can move mountains and achieve the unprecedented.

Vallakottai Temple — King Bhagirathan

King Bhagirathan was well-known and famous. But he had a very bad habit of not respecting others. One day he encountered a situation which cost him all the wealth of his Kingdom.

It seems that one day King Bhagirathan was camping with his army. At that time Sage Narada came to see the king. As was customary, Narada greeted Bhagirathan, but Bhagirathan did not return the greeting. Bhagirathan thought to himself that since he was a King and Narada was just a saint well... perhaps the greeting was unnecessary. In fact, he ignored Narada even further by looking away, in another direction.

Narada was hurt by the behavior of Bhagirathan and certainly didn't expect this kind of behavior from a king. He left the place and continued his journey. On the way Narada met an asura called Koran. Koran greeted Narada and welcomed him. He offered him a very warm welcome. Narada was pleased by the behavior of Koran. Accordingly, Narada was able to find good qualities in Koran—qualities which the king, Bhagirathan, seemed to lack.

Koran had so far defeated ninety-nine kings and mentioned to Narada that he was looking to beat another king in order to make it one hundred. "If he wins over one hundred kings", he said, "then he will be granted extraordinary status, both with boons and with some amazing powers". Narada, now aware of this, suddenly thought of King Bhagirathan and the lesson he might teach him. Narada, therefore, told Koran that he could easily defeat Bhagirathan and, in doing so, accomplish his hundredth victory.

Narada also told him where Bhagirathan was camping and that it was very near their current location. Koran then began to wage a war with King Bhagirathan. Inevitably, Bhagirathan couldn't stand the might of Koran and lost. Finally Bhagirathan was left with nothing. He lost his kingdom and all the riches.

Bhagirathan immediately felt sorry for not respecting Narada and so realized his mistake. As soon as he could, he met with Narada. He fell at Narada's feet and begged for forgiveness.

Narada felt sorry and asked Bhagirathan to meet Sage Durvasa who could possibly help him.

As advised by Narada, Bhagirathan begged Durvasa to tell him a way in which he might get his kingdom and dignity back. Durvasa advised Bhagirathan to worship Lord Murugan. Further, he asked Bhagirathan to find a place where Murugan resides under a holy *Patiri* (Bignonia) tree with his two consorts. He also asked him to fast on Fridays. Bhagirathan thanked Durvasa and went in search of Lord Murugan.

Bhagirathan wandered for a long time trying to find the right place. Finally he came to a place called Kottainagar. There he found Murugan residing under the *Patiri* tree with his two consorts as foretold. He stayed there for a long time. He prayed to Murugan every day asking to regain his lost glory. He fasted on Fridays and was sincere and true with his prayers.

Murugan was pleased with his prayers and appeared to Bhagirathan. He blessed him and gave Bhagirathan back his lost wealth and glory. Since then Bhagirathan became a devout follower of Murugan and spent most of his time spreading Lord Murugan's glories to this world. He went on to build many temples for Lord Murugan, including one in the place where Lord Murugan first appeared to him (now Vallakottai Murugan Temple).

Legend of Alappad Temple

One of Murugan's most enduring legends can be found in a small town of Alappad, though the story has its origins in the Puranas.

Apart from his warrior-god image, Murugan has a very playful nature. In fact, once he even committed a very silly error that angered his father, Lord Shiva. Shiva, known to anger quickly, actually curses Murugan to be born as a fish. Murugan's mother, goddess Parvati, was sad at her son's fate so she asked Shiva to forgive his son. But this only infuriated Shiva further and he then cursed Parvati to be born as a fisherwoman. But after his anger cooled a bit, Lord Shiva promised to liberate both Murugan and Parvati and bless them at an appropriate time.

In keeping with the curse, Murugan assumed the form of a fish but he went one step further and assumed the form of a huge whale. He caused terrible trouble to the fisherman of Alappad by tearing their nets and overturning their boats, so they could no longer go fishing and were robbed of their livelihood.

The poor fishermen were forced to starve and went to their King but he could not find a solution either. In fact the king's treasury went bankrupt after feeding all the starving people. In desperation the king announced that whoever catches the troublesome whale must be rewarded with a marriage to the King's beautiful daughter.

But since the whale was huge and fearsome nobody dared to take up the challenge until an old man appeared from the north. His back was bent as a bow due to his age but he still boldly approached the King saying he could capture the whale. This was Lord Shiva in disguise. The King and his subjects, though astonished, accompanied the old man to the sea. The old man then made a huge rope by twisting many lines together and holding one end in his hand, threw the other into the sea. The whale, lying submerged in the water, became entangled in the lines and the old man instructed the fishermen to pull the rope with all their strength while chanting a *mantra* he taught them.

After hours of hard work finally the whale was pulled to the shore but the people were in for a divine treat because the whale had completely vanished. In its place stood Lord Murugan—completely freed from Shiva's curse. The thankful King and subjects built a temple for Lord Murugan where the great whale was shored. The temple at Alappad still stands to this day, housing a huge whale statue.

The King, who had promised to marry his beautiful daughter to the man who caught the whale, was in a real quandary. He would not break his promise but could not bear to see his daughter married to the old man. But the people of Alappad believed that a verbal promise should always be upheld and while the King hesitated, his daughter who was goddess Parvati came forward and said yes to the proposal. So she walked away with the old man while people kept asking where they were going. They both replied they have no particular place and kept walking until they reached a spot where they both turned into statues. This place came to be called Chenganoor.

Years later, at the site where the temple for Murugan was built, a strange phenomenon occurred which made the people of Alappad consult their religious thinking. Whenever water from the pond was drawn for abhishekam there was always a fish present in the water. Finally people learned of the curse and started making the appropriate arrangements.

They realized that the old man and the beautiful princess were never married in a ceremony so the people of Alappad (where Parvati was born) take her dowry and go to Chenganoor to conduct the divine marriage. This custom continues today and attracts thousands of devotees every year. It is believed if the local people try to skip the marriage celebrations even for a year, unexplained natural calamities take place. So the ritual continues and people who are believed to be cursed also pray to Lord Murugan for the removal of that curse.

This story illustrates that, over the aeons, Murugan plays out various leelas for the benefit of his devotees. He may do it on his own or with the help of his parents as demonstrated in this story.

MURUGAN ABHISHEKAM

All Murugan temples have rituals that are performed for the benefit of devotees and one of the most important one is the 'abhishekam'; the bathing, or lovingly daubing, the idol of the deity. The reason for the abhishekam becomes important because it is the material and physical way a devotee can relate to Murugan and realize the 'touch' sense of the body. When the idol is bathed or smeared using different materials (such as milk, fruit, honey, or butter), a part of it is saved, mixed in a bowl and is given away to the devotees in the form of a 'prasadam', for consumption. As the devotee eats the 'prasadam' he/she 'touches' a physical part of Murugan and also absorbs the vibration and the energy of the idol and thereby assimilates the energy of the primordial force itself.

The Murugan idol at Palani has special properties since it's made from 'nava pashanam' (nine medicinal herbs) and eating the 'Panchamritham' used for the idol's abhishekam has medicinal values too. It cures many diseases, especially of the skin. Even the water that is used to wash the idol of the Lord becomes sacred and is used to anoint oneself to wash away sins and physical illness.

In temples, watching the process of abhishekam itself is a divine experience as devotees forget the outside world and watch their favorite god being washed with water, curd, honey, butter, ghee (clarified butter) or milk. One's ego takes a rest and oneness with Murugan is attained for those precious moments while watching the abhishekam being performed. When the prasadam is consumed with uttermost faith and devotion it cures many diseases of the body and mind. Abhishekam of Murugan is not done just to 'purify' the idol but it is done for the purification of his devotees. During abhishekam, *mantras* to Murugan are also recited in unison and the vibrations from these sounds bring peace to the mind of a devotee.

While abhishekam is for the purification of the body, mind and soul it also has worldly purpose. Abhishekam can also be performed to bring peace and prosperity. Abhishekam can be used to gain wealth, health and prosperity in the world and is performed by devotees praying to Murugan.

There are different materials that can be used for abhishekam and each has its own significance and importance. Gingili oil abhishekam ensures good health, as rice flour gives relief from debts. While a mix of abhishekam materials can cure ailments, saffron powder is used to gain attractive looks. Holy water such as the waters of river Ganges is used for prosperity. Ghee abhishekam is used for salvation, while milk ensures long life.

Panchakaviyam and Panchamritham abhishekam are done to gain purity and success, respectively. It is believed an abhishekam performed with milk and curd helps a couple have healthy babies while honey is used for health, intelligence and musical talents.

Bathing Murugan idol with sugarcane juices frees the body from illness and using brown sugar can ensure success over enemies. Using banana fruit for abhishekam means a good crop harvest and using mango fruit again promotes healthy offspring.

Using pomegranate fruits for Murugan abhishekam will calm down anger and oranges makes a person impartial. Lime fruits are used to overcome fear of death and cooked rice for gaining the gift of a kingdom. Tender coconut water is used to enjoy the pleasures of life and vibhuthi abhishekam is done to obtain intelligence. Sandal pastes make one wealthy and KumKum (red vermillion) ensures prosperity. To be free from fear, scented water is used and sweet-rice abhishekam is performed to be free from famine.

SHANMUGA BHUJANGAM: AADI

SHANKARACHARYA

Lord Murugan has been present from time immemorial but traditions and cultures over the ages have given him various names and forms. He has been worshipped by one and all to gain various powers. While Murugan in Palani is mainly known for his mystical quality and renunciation he can also be invoked for gaining wealth and good health.

Amongst his six battle houses Tiruchendur is known as the 'house of victory' because this is where he camped during the epic battle against the asuras. Over the eons the temple built at this mythological and historical site has gained importance for other reasons, too.

Various Murugan devotees like Arunagirinathar, who wrote the famous Thiruppugazh in praise of Lord Murugan, visited this place and wrote about its importance in his works. Pagazhi, (aka Pakalli) Koottar (1762 A.D.) a Vaishnava saint, was cured of a stomach ache after praying to Tiruchendur Murugan and composed a brilliant work called Pillai Tamil. A more detailed account of Pakalli is presented in this book. Kandasamy Pulavar (1736—1760 A.D.) a great Murugan devotee regained his lost sight after praying here. But the most important work of all 'The Shanmukha Bhujangam' which was written by Sri Aadi

116

Shankaracharya was also composed at Tiruchendur and has a very fascinating story behind it.

The birth and legend of Aadi Shankaracharya itself is steeped in mystery and divinity. Some 2,500 years ago, there lived a childless couple Sivaguru and his wife Aryambal in Kaladi, Kerala. They travelled to Trichur to pray for a son. They performed the forty eight day pooja to the presiding deity Lord Shiva who was known as Vadakkunathan. Pleased with their devotion and prayers, Lord Shiva appeared and asked the couple if they wanted many dull sons or one brilliant son with a short lifespan. The devout couple answered they cannot make a decision because only the Lord knows what is good for them.

Pleased with their answer Lord Dakshinamurthy, another 'wise incarnation' of Shiva, was born to Aryambal as a son under the 'Thiruvaithirai' star. They named him Shankara, who later became the great ascetic and Sage Sri Aadi Shankaracharya.

Aadi Shankara travelled all over India preaching the Hindu philosophy and he has written many prayers and hymns praising various gods like Shiva, Vishnu, and Brahma, and also goddesses like Durga, Lakshmi and Saraswati. But his 'stotra' (hymn) on Lord Murugan stands out because it can be sung or recited even today to cure oneself of various diseases.

When Aadi Shankara came to Tiruchendur he suffered a severe stomach ache, so one night he ate the sacred vibhuthi in a leaf which is offered to Lord Murugan. After eating the ash he was miraculously cured of his pain. That is when he composed the 'Shanmukha Bhujangam' for the benefit of others.

Some of the verses of the Shanmukha Bhujangam have such beautiful lines and meaning that reciting them gives a joy that is beyond compare. One verse reads *"I do not know the science of musical sounds, or the meaning of complex text. I do not know the nature of shlokas or padaas, or the intricacy of the gadhyam. But my heart shines with the effulgent light of six luminous faces. Because of which my mouth sings amazing praises with musical tone and extempore meanings"*.

There are thirty three verses in the 'Shanmukha Bhujangam' and each verse praises different aspects and manifestations of Lord Murugan. Each verse, while praising a body part of Murugan, ends with asking Murugan to protect that body part in the human body.

Aadi Shankaracharya also wrote other hymns about Lord Murugan like the 'Subrahmanya Karavalambashtakam,' and 'Subrahmanya Pancha Rathan'. 'Skanda Shashti Kavacham' was composed by Devaraya Swamigal and Paamban Swamigal composed the 'Shanmukha Kavacham' in the year 1891.

118

The end of the Shanmukha Bhujangam itself says that the one who worships with devotion the great Guha by reading the poems in the Bhujangam style, will be blessed with good sons, a wife, wealth, long life and will attain eternal bliss with Skanda.

People even today recite the Shanmukha Bhujangam and Shanmukha Kavacham for relief from different diseases. Even while receiving modern medical treatment, only people who have faith in the medicines and genuinely believe that they will be cured, are found to be freed from diseases. The great works of yesteryear operate the same way.

VEL – THE MARVELOUS SPEAR OF MURUGAN

Murugan is known to use a divine spear (or javelin) called the vel. Although Tamilians in ancient times also used a spear for the purpose of warfare, as far as the story of Murugan's marvelous vel goes, this spear became synonymous with valor and signifies good triumphing over evil simply by being touched by Murugan.

Once, the Kailasha mountain abode of Lord Shiva and Murugan was visited by other deities—Brahma, Indra, even Vishnu. They came to Lord Shiva and reported monstrous demonic (Asura) deeds; acts of cruelty on the innocent.

Besides reporting this, they prayed to Lord Shiva to put an end to the tyranny. Murugan was asked by Lord Shiva to combat the asuras with his army to put an end to the sufferings faced by the gods. While commanding him thus, Lord Shiva blessed Murugan as he embarked upon the task of annihilating Surapadman along with his brothers.

In other versions of the story, it is said that the vel was gifted by Parvati. They say the vel was presented by goddess Parvati to her son Murugan as a symbol or embodiment of her power for vanquishing Surapadman, an asura who was harassing the gods.

In the Kanda Purana, Murugan's war with Surapadman and his evil forces is described in detail. The legend declares that when it was clear to the asura that defeat was at hand, he transformed into a giant mango tree under the ocean so as to keep Murugan from detecting him. Murugan, ever vigilant, saw through this disguise and hurled the vel at the mango tree which immediately split into two halves.

Out of the two halves, one was transformed into a peacock (or Mayil) and the other became a rooster (or Seval). Murugan started using the peacock as his vehicle (or vahana) while his battle flag flaunted the emblem of the rooster. Thus did the spear help in attaining the triumph of good over evil and is now synonymous with valor. The story also goes on to present his compassion that even after defeating his enemy he elevates the enemy to glory and inducts him into his service.

On the spiritual front, the vel of discrimination annihilates the inner enemies (or the evils of Karma, Avidya and Kama) and in the process helps in the liberation of life in transmigration. Saint Arunagirinathar refers to the marvelous spear of Murugan as one with mysterious power. In one of the Thiruppugal songs written by Saint Arunagirinathar, the divine spear is referred to as the *Mantra Vel*.

The vel looks like a lance and is triangular in shape; it is sharp, and blessed, it is always held with the tip pointing upwards in the direction of the sky (heaven). This weapon is considered sacred. The rooster and the peacock are the other attributes closely associated with Murugan as also is the mace or staff as held in the Dandayudhapani form in Palani. The instrument used for slaying demons as per the Vedas, is also a symbol of the penetration of wisdom and spiritual knowledge by cutting away ignorance.

Each year in Southern India a procession is organized in honor of Murugan. Miniature lances are used by devotees for piercing parts of the body during the procession. A very famous Murugan temple, thirteen kilometers away from Vellore was built in honor of Murugan around five thousand years ago. This becomes the seat of activity during the festival.

The story of the vel and its association with Lord Shiva's son is symbolic of the message in the Vedas saying that, shortcomings must be combatted and won over for the pristine soul to find liberation. This can only be accomplished with the sharpness of intellect; in essence, a vel ingrained in all humans.

SARAVANA POIGAI

The birth of Murugan has its roots even before Skanda Purana. Skanda is also believed to be the incarnation of Sanatha Kumara. In the very beginning of this universe,

Brahma created four spiritual children namely Sanak, Sanandan, Sanatana and Sanatha Kumara. Even by the age of three, Sanatha Kumara exhibited divine wisdom and was way beyond his age. This amazed the devatas and even Lord Shiva who had heard about the child and went to meet and bless him. Shiva was so impressed with the child he asked the child to ask for any kind of boon. But Sanatha Kumara said he had nothing to ask and wanted to know if Lord Shiva wanted any kind of boon instead! This impressed Lord Shiva so much that he asked the child to be born as his son. But the child had another condition, he said he did not want to be born out of a womb and wanted to be born as an 'Ayonija' (or a being born without the participation of the female womb).

In the meantime, the asuras had started creating havoc in Devaloka, and the devatas, who knew that only the son of Shiva could bring about destruction of the asuras, went seeking Lord Shiva's help, who happened to be deep in meditation.

As recounted in the first chapter, when Shiva opened his third eye (out of which six sparks emerged), the sparks were too powerful for even Agni (the fire god) to carry, so he asked for help from Ganga Devi. She in turn carried the sparks and placed them on six lotuses in a small pond called "Sarvana Poigai". Each spark then turned into a beautiful child and was cared for by celestial maidens called "Krittikas'. When Shiva's consort, goddess Parvati heard this she went to Saravana Poigai and united all the six babies into one child with six heads and twelve arms. Thus Murugan was born without the help of a womb and he embodies the wisdom of Sanatha Kumara and the knowledge of his father and the 'shakti' of his mother. He also has the beauty of the love god Manmatha of eternal youth.

The place that Murugan was born literally translates into 'born of the forest of reeds' and so the main *mantra* for Murugan is 'Sharavana Bhava'. The six syllables that form the *mantra* also stands for the six Krittikas who looked after him. He is also called Karthikeya or the one cared for by Krittikas. One of the major festivals for Karthikeya is also called Aadi Karthikai, celebrated during the month of 'Aadi' (15 July – 15 August). Since the maidens took care of the divine baby, Lord Shiva and Devi Parvati blessed them, saying that a special day will be celebrated in their memory. Karthikeya hence, bears their Nakashatram (star) as his birth star 'Krithiga or Krittika' or Pleiades constellation.

Though the original pool is located in the Himalayas, Lord Murugan's temple in Tiru Avinakudi also has a similar pool. Devotees believe that taking a dip in the pool cures various skin diseases and people take a dip in the pool even to this day before entering the temple premises. All sins are meant to be washed away after a dip here.

Rahul Kabade

The Murugan temple at Thiruparankundram also has a 'Saravana Poigai' pond on its premises. The great Murugan devotee and poet Nakkirar stood in the pond while singing praises to Murugan.

There is also a Saravana Poigai in the Murugan temple at Tiruttani and it is believed that taking a bath in its holy water cures people of mental ailments and gives peace of mind. Tiruttani was the place where Lord Murugan himself found peace after his battle with Surapadman. This also shows that even ponds with reeds can be transformed into sacred water by the power of Murugan. He is known to convert useless things into the most useful things for his followers.

SHANMUKHA AND THE NUMBER SIX

The different names of Lord Murugan have different meanings and significance but they all lead to one path—enlightenment. Murugan personifies beauty, eternal youth and fragrance but as Aarumughan—the six faced one there is a deeper esoteric meaning.

The name Shanmughan (Sanskrit) and Aarumughan (Tamil) have similar meaning, while in Sanskrit the 'Shad' stands for the numeral six and mughan or mukham means face. In Tamil, the word 'Aaru' has different meanings, like the number six, or a river, or a path and even 'time'.

Arunagirinathar the Tamil poet, who wrote the 'Thiruppugazh' in praise of Murugan, starts the first verse with the name "Aarumughan" repeated six times. The reason for this is because the number six and the word 'Aaru' have deeper esoteric meanings. The word Aaru stands for the stages and ways to achieve a goal while the 'mughan' stands for face, the gateway, or the junction.

So as Aarumughan Murugan has six faces and the ability to see in all four directions and also the upper world of the celestial beings and the inner world of the human soul, this makes Him 'all-pervading' and omnipresent. His six faces also denote the five faces of Shiva (his father) and one face of his mother (Parvati).

The number six also occurs in various stages of Murugan's life, he is cared for by six Krittikas' or celestial maidens. He camped at six places during the battle against asuras and though he is all-pervasive he manifests the strongest in his six temples.

The 'Kundalini Yoga' which talks about the awakening of the 'Kundalini Shakti' in the human body has six *chakras* or stages and once the 'Kundru' (power) reaches the top-most chakra (Sixth Sahasrara Chakra)—the head of the human body— 'Aarumughan' dances there with joy; meaning oneness with Brahman is attained. Murugan has to camp at the six *chakras* in the body to overcome the six enemies before peace and bliss can be attained. Only after which, does He, as 'Aarumughan', stand for 'Aaru-dhal' or peace.

The '*Surasamharam*' or destruction or transformation of the asura Surapadman took place on the sixth day of the waxing moon in the month of 'Aippasi' (November) and so Kanda Shashti is celebrated on the sixth day, after fasting for six days.

Although idols are used in all temples for worship most of the Hindu deities also have geometrical figures as the symbolic

127

representation of their power. This figure is referred to as 'Yantra' or *'Chakras'*. They are so called because they indicate completeness and active movement. Aarumughan's Yantra has six corners or two over-lapping triangles with six sides, again highlighting the play of number six in the depiction of Lord Murugan. Aarumughan's moola (main) *mantra* also has six letters 'sa ra va na ba va'.

But apart from this, the number six and Aarumughan's life story, there is the story of every human being. Every human body is conceived in a watery/fluid environment (i.e. Ganga) and develops in the womb or 'sarvanam' and has six senses— the sixth being intuition which represents the power of Murugan.

Though every human being has inborn divine powers like the seed of a tree, they have to reach god by destroying Surapadman, i.e. the six internal enemies of anger, delusion, arrogance, lust, avarice and envy.

This shows that realizing the inner workings of Murugan's power and understanding the power within a human soul is the way to salvation. Learning to 'read between the lines' is one aspect of devotion that every Murugan devotee is expected to learn early in life because Murugan is predominantly mystical in his manifestations. As one learns to peel away the various

Rahul Kabade

layers in the meanings of Murugan's name, symbols, depictions and yantras, he/she also learns the lessons of life and the unfolding of the Universe within themselves.

KACHIYAPPA SIVACHARIAR AND MURUGAN

One fine day Murugan appeared to Kachiyappa Sivachariar in a dream and ordered him to sing in Tamil the Kantha (Kanda) Purana. This he would have to do after getting it translated from Sankara Samhita, a Sanskrit work. And this was not all. Murugan also told him that the first lines of the song have to be 'Tigadachakkara-chemmukha-maindullan'.

Accordingly, on waking he began thinking about it over and over again. He considered this task as a supreme directive from Murugan and engaged in this activity with humility and care. Every day Kachiyappa would first write the accounts of Murugan's career when he would feel inspired and at the Murugan Subrahmanya idol in Kumara Kottam, the entire day's work would be deposited with reverence and devotion.

And then there were miracles! Every night the manuscript written by Kachiyappa was modified by Murugan and the corrections were visible. It is for this reason that the Kanda Purana is regarded as the ultimate account on Murugan. It is believed to be authoritative for the very good reason that Murugan himself inspired and corrected it.

The first line mentioned in the account was something of which many of the Pundits (scholars) wanted an interpretation. This anxious desire of the Pundits came at a time when the

130

account was read for recognition before a large assembly. They would not believe that Kachiyappa had overall authority and contested the grammar. While this debate was happening, Kachiyappa was in tears and praying for Murugan's help. By the grace of Murugan, one of the Pundits in the assembly came to his rescue and suggested that in the type of grammar found in Kachiyappa's work could only come from the Tamil work Virasolliyam, a work that was very ancient. This development was regarded as divine by all scholars present in the assembly and accordingly the work became authoritative. Many of the people among Tamil audiences were already very well acquainted with Murugan's power, which was truly marvelous and one that was unquestionably rich in reward.

The Virasolliyam, in its original form, was intended to be recited aloud to these audiences. Kanda Puranam's version is intended to be read as well as viewed by devotees, both old and young, across the globe. This piece of work does not know far or near, it is pure bliss as stated in the Puranam. Scriptures state that simply by beholding this account, everyone is sure to obtain Murugan's grace.

He is considered to be the fountainhead of Tamil literature in three branches, namely: theatre, verse, and prose, and is also hailed as the repository of knowledge.

Kachiyappa Sivachariar is believed to be close to Murugan's heart. In fact, many devotional and priceless songs in Tamil praise Murugan and sing of his glories. The story of Kachiyappa Sivachariar's tears in the assembly of Pundits being challenged and put through severe test is synonymous with the experience of many Murugan devotees.

A diamond has to first go through extreme treatment, and then must be chiseled even further to bring out the fire within so that it may eventually be polished to shine. In the same way a true devotee is challenged and put to an extreme test by Murugan to make the devotee's human birth a celebrated one.

Rahul Kabade

THE STORY OF ARUNAGIRINATHAR

The life history of the Sage Arunagirinathar, a Tamil poet, illustrates the point perfectly that "every sinner has a future and every saint has a past". He was born into a traditional and devout Hindu family in the 14th century in Tiruvannamalai, a small town in Tamil Nadu.

Even if no definite texts are available of the entire account of Arunagirinathar, the word-of-mouth legends told over the centuries all recount the same story. His father passed away as soon as the baby was born and his elder sister and mother raised him, instilling the traditional values of family and religion. When the boy was seven years old his mother passed away too leaving him in the care of his elder sister Adhi, after extracting a promise that she will do nothing to displease her younger brother.

As Arunagiri grew he completely neglected his studies and enjoyed the company of women. He squandered away the family's wealth as well as his sister's money and ornaments. Finally when there was nothing left, the frustrated sister suggested that he should sell her body to meet his demands. This had such a profound effect on Arunagiri that he ran to the Tiruvannamalai temple to throw himself off from the tower shouting Muruga! Muruga! Muruga! Nobody can understand the mysteries of Murugan for before Arunagiri reached the ground his beloved Murugan was standing below to catch him!

A few scholars may object to the glorification of Arunagirinathar's early life saying it sanctions vice and other malpractices. But a deeper study reveals that, although the sage had this weakness for women, otherwise he was quite well versed in scholarly works of the time.

In his writings he shows his knowledge in ancient Tamil works like 'Tevaram', 'Thirukurral', 'Madal', 'Malai' and other ancient works. His song about 'archana' (worship) on Murugan is written mostly in Sanskrit which only means he was well versed in Sanskrit and Tamil. He also knew much about the Puranas, Gita, Upanishads and Agamas as is reflected in his work.

The 'Thiruppugazh' which means 'Glory of Murugan' is a beautiful composition of hymns in praise of Murugan. Though originally the Sage wrote 16,000 hymns, only around 1,300 are available now. It was Arunagirinathar who brought into practice the art of worshipping god with songs and not *mantras* which had originally been the norm.

The "Kandar Anubhuthi'—here Kandar is Murugan and Anubhuthi means 'god attainment'—was written by Arunagirinathar and is a direct account of his experiences with Skanda and is considered as his best work. The work also provides a path to other seekers to experience the power of Murugan. Though Arunagirinathar wrote songs in praise of his favorite god, he cleverly brought in other deities like Shiva, Vishnu, Parvati, and Ganesha into his songs by citing their relation to his beloved Kanda (Skanda).

Apart from Thiruppugazh and Kandar Anubhuthi, the Sage Arunagirinathar also produced beautiful works like Kandar Alangaram, Thiru Vaguppu, Mayil Viruththam, Kandar Anthaathi, Seval Viruththam, Vel Viruththam, and Thiru Velu Kootrirukkai, which are still sung in all Murugan temples. They are also used by devotees in their personal prayers to Murugan.

Although his works speak volumes about his devotion to Murugan, his earlier life and his attempted suicide hold an interesting lesson for all to learn. Murugan does not intervene in every suicide attempt but Arunagirinathar was granted this highest form of compassion, the reason being, he realized the important truth that his body had failed to serve the purpose for which it was made. Though his sister's words triggered the ultimate shame and realization, he had already failed in many attempts to reform earlier.

According to the many shastras (knowledge based on timeless principles) the last thought at the moment of death is very important in a person's life because that determines his or her rebirth. Taking the name of Vishnu or Shiva ensures *moksha* but Arunagirinathar understood the fundamental failure of his body, so he decided to end his life, that moment of truth saved him.

From leading a life of debauchery to then becoming a man of devotion and piety with the grace of Murugan the impossible can be achieved. The six-faced Shanmukha can transform anyone with his grace and compassion. This story shows that true transformation can happen only with divine grace. God's compassion is infinite. He puts us in the best possible situation in life to learn and grow and eventually reach Him (Super soul).

VALLI'S MARRIAGE

In the Skanda Purana, Murugan is shown as an eternal bachelor or sometimes He is said to be married to Indra's daughter Devasena or Deviyani. But the Kanda Puranam gives more importance to the second bride of Murugan, the hunter-girl, Valli.

The story of Valli is fascinating and starts with a hunter named Nambi who lives in a village beneath the Valli Malai. Here the meaning of Valli is yam and Malai is mountain. Nambi Raj, who is also the tribe's leader, has only male children and longs for a female child. A sage named Sivamuni also lives on the mountain slope leading a life of austerity. One day a beautiful gazelle passes by him and the sage is so captivated by the gazelle that his lascivious thoughts make her pregnant. But there is another fascinating aspect to this because the embryo is none other than the daughter of Mal, who had done penance and taken a vow to marry Murugan, in her previous life.

The gazelle, after giving birth to the human child, abandons her in a pit dug by the hunter-tribe's women in the forest when they were in search of valli (a yam). When the women find a beautiful girl-child they take her to their chief. Nambi and his wife are only too happy to bring up the baby girl and name her Valli since she was found in the valli pit. From a very young

137

age Valli dedicates her heart and soul to her beloved god, Murugan, and constantly expresses her desire to be with Him. When she is twelve years of age, Valli goes to the millet field to guard it. She sits on an elevated platform called 'paran' chasing away the birds that come to eat the grains.

Murugan, who is pleased with her sincere love and dedication, assumes the form of a hunter and tries to woo the girl with his leela, but she rebukes him. Valli warns him that the hunters are wild men and may harm him. Later, Murugan assumes the form of an old man and asks for food, Valli offers him millet and honey and even quenches his thirst by fetching water from a pond nearby. The old man then tells Valli since she helped satisfy his hunger and thirst, she should now also satisfy his need for love. Valli, of course, is shocked so Murugan still in disguise as the old man enlists his elder brother Ganesha's help to frighten Valli, in the form of a rampaging elephant. Valli who is scared of the elephant pleads to the old man to save her but the old man insists that she promise to marry him first, and in the heat of the moment she says yes. Murugan then reveals his true form to her and Valli is only too happy to find out it was her beloved Murugan who played the prank. In the spiritual sense, Lord Ganesha's presence is essential for completing the matrimonial rites.

They enjoy a blissful courtship but soon the harvest season is over and Valli has to return to her home. Her mother notices

Rahul Kabade

her unhappiness and asks her the reason but Valli refuses to reveal her secret affair with her beloved Murugan.

The next day Murugan, who looks for Valli in the fields, is distraught to find her missing so he goes to the village and elopes with her. The hunter tribesmen wage a battle to bring Valli back. A fierce battle ensues, in which the hunter-tribesmen are all killed but Valli persuades Murugan to forgive them and grant back their life. Murugan agrees and finally Valli and Murugan are united in holy matrimony with the blessings of the hunter-tribe who later realize that the groom is none other than their 'Kula swami' (family deity).

By assuming the form of a human and undergoing love pangs and asking for help from his brother, Murugan showed that any amount of obstacles can be overcome if we are resilient and have pure love in our hearts. Valli is also known as the 'Ichha Shakti' (will power or power of aspirations) and along with Murugan's vel which is the 'Jnana Shakti' (wisdom or power of knowledge) and Deviyani who is also the 'Kriya Shakti' (power of action), she forms an integral part of Murugan and his divine power.

The importance of taking a vow is also demonstrated in this story. When Valli vows to marry Murugan, and no one else, she is ready to undergo trials and tribulations to reach her goal. That is the reason why people still continue with a *moun vrata* (vow of silence), or the *oru pozdhu* (the fasting vow)

Sri Muruga

even to this day, so that they may accomplish their everyday
goals.

NINE BROTHERS OF MURUGAN

The purpose of Murugan's birth is truly interesting because he was born to destroy evil and restore order. But it starts with a damsel named Maya who is from the clan of asuras. She is clever, cunning, and also knows many magical tricks. She once went to a great sage called Kashyapa and served him while he did his penance. The sage, out of gratitude, offered her a boon she wanted but Maya, being clever, tricked him and asked the sage to father her children.

Maya and the sage had three sons Surapadman, Simhamukhan, Tarakasuran and a daughter called Ajamukhi. Many other asuras were also born from the sweat of the three asuras. The asuras studied under their powerful guru Shukracharya who taught them many *mantras* while their mother taught them magical tricks. She also advised her sons to do intense penance to obtain Shiva's blessings.

While Tarakasuran had a boon from Brahma, Surapadman did a rigorous penance that pleased Shiva and was granted a boon of life for 108 Yugas and to be a ruler of one thousand and eight kingdoms. Once Surapadman realized he was practically invincible, he and his brothers started to terrorize the devatas. They conquered Devaloka and made the devatas their servants. The devatas were petrified but nobody had the courage and strength to stand up against Surapadman and his army of asuras. The devatas knew that only the power of Shiva's as-yet-unborn son could destroy Surapadman but were afraid to approach Shiva. After Murugan was born, he was looked after by the Krittikas and grew under Shiva and Parvati's love and care. However, the parents also wanted to help Murugan accomplish his purpose. Once when the anklet (chilambu) of Parvati broke, nine gems rolled out. With the help of Shiva, Parvati turned these nine gems into nine powers (Shakti's) or nine warriors (Nava Veera). They came to be the nine brothers of Murugan. All of them had names that started with Veera (brave/warrior) and the chief and most famous of them was Veerabahu. The eight other brothers were called Veerakesari, Veera Mahendran, Veera Maheswaran, Veera Rakshan, Veera Marthandan, Veerandhagan, Veeradheeran and Veera Suran.

When Murugan later became the celestial army chief in the fight against Surapadman and his sons and brothers, He had help from his own brothers too. During the fight between Surapadman and the celestial army, Veerabahu leads an army and goes to the Krauncha mountains. Murugan also sent Veerabahu as messenger to Mahendrapuri, the Capitol of asuras. He went to meet Surapadman at Attani mandapam with Murugan's message asking Surapadman to surrender. But Surapadman insulted Veerabahu by not offering him a seat. With the grace of Murugan a throne decorated with precious gems appeared and Veerabahu sat on it and praised

142

Murugan's greatness. But Surapadman only laughed and asked his men to throw Veerabahu in prison, since it was considered a sin to kill a messenger. However, Veerabahu destroyed Attani mandapam and also killed Satamukhan and Vakshiravagu the sons of Surapadman and several other asuras.

Veerabahu also tamed a ram that escapes from the *Yagna* fires of Narada Muni. When it goes on a rampage Murugan asks his brother to find it and Veerabahu brings it back to Murugan and the ram becomes Murugan's vehicle for a short period.

Another very endearing story of the love and affection between Murugan and Veerabahu is demonstrated when Brahma comes visiting Kailasha. When Murugan asks the meaning of the sacred Om, Brahma answers that He himself is Om, hearing this Veerabahu is filled with rage and clenching his fist hits Brahma's head. Subsequently Murugan imprisons Brahma. Love and affection between brothers and the importance of family in the Hindu diaspora emanates from such divine tales.

Once, Veerabahu defeats Surapadman's son, Bhanugopan. Pleased by this act Murugan offers Veerabahu a boon. Veerabahu asks for a boon of unwavering devotion to Murugan, which is granted. Upon granting this boon, Murugan said that such a boon has never been given even to the devatas.

MURUGAN – TAMIL GOD OF JUSTICE

The Hindu pantheon is known for the numerous deities, sub-deities and folk deities who have evolved and changed over a period of time. The primary or main deities, Shiva—Parvati, Vishnu—Lakshmi, Brahma—Saraswati, Ganesha and Skanda have been present from time immemorial. But the stories that explain their origin, function, character, valor and courage are used to instruct people on the purpose of life and the workings of the Universe.

The story of Murugan who was born from the light or spark that emanated when Lord Shiva opened his third eye has a special and unique place in the ancient stories and history of India as in all the South Asian countries in which he is worshipped.

Though Murugan is known as the 'worthy son of Shiva' and is worshipped all over India, in the present Yuga, he is predominantly known as the "Tamizh Kaduval" (Tamil god). The cultural and religious lives of Tamilians around the world revolve around their favorite deity, Murugan. The old Sangam literature uses Murugan as an example to explain many aspects of life like valor, justice, mercy, wisdom, beauty, unity, and the destruction of dark forces.

The concept of justice that has evolved in the tribal and Tamil tradition is not some abstract concept. They use Murugan to explain the concept of valor and justice. This is because of Murugan's accessibility to a wide range of people and different sects. He can be physically experienced by people.

Murugan, no matter in which form, is depicted as the one who brings order into the chaos of the Universe. As Skanda he was commander-in-chief of the celestial army and as a deity of justice he brings order into the everyday life of devotees. Like a good king he punishes sins and bad deeds but he also transforms a person from within to bring out the inherent good qualities of a person.

In the Sangam period and subsequent period that Tamil culture has evolved, bravery in protecting one's tribe, personal wealth and cattle were held in the highest esteem. Murugan represented that protective aspect for most tribes. The brave men who gave up their lives to protect life and property were rewarded with head stones or spears in the villages.

But Murugan is also part of the non-physical form of bravery, valor, and justice. The '*Cur*' is part of Tamil culture and it represents the abstract form of fear which dwells in the forests and mountains. The local tribal gods were not considered strong enough to fight the Cur. Murugan (as Velan) is the human god of justice who can fight the Cur and ensure justice for the people around different villages and mountains.

Though *Cur* is vague and abstract it actually represents the suffering, terror, fear, and natural disasters that happen in the Universe. Murugan with his bravery and man-like character was seen to be best suited to protect all people from the Cur. Cur is not limited to one area or region, it affects everyone and Murugan was also not limited to one area or tribe. He is present everywhere in all directions as signified by his six faces and he was the perfect match for the Cur. He could overcome it with his Shakti vel. Thus the legend of Murugan as the Tamil god of justice grew and today he is worshipped to ensure that justice.

Accordingly, Murugan today is invoked to ensure justice is done to an individual on a personal level as well. The Tiruchendur temple in Tamil Nadu sees scores of devotees thronging to it every day and more so, on festivals like Thaipusam and Kanda Shashti because people still believe Murugan helps people settle scores with their enemies.

In tribal and community worship, Murugan is worshipped as the Kula swami but he is also a personal god who can be asked for help anytime. The Shanmukha Bhujamgam and Kanda Shashti Kavacham are recited even today for protection from an enemy and to ensure justice is delivered on an individual level.

Murugan may be present from the beginning as a warrior-god because he is portrayed as young, handsome and fond of

146

blood sacrifices. But in Tamil Nadu he is also known as the god of justice. Tamilians believe that Murugan always delivers justice for his devotees. He can be called on by a group of people, a tribe or just an individual, his accessibility is Murugan's most salient feature as a personal god of justice.

MURUGAN AND HIS VOW OF CELIBACY

Though in the Dravidian and Tamil culture Murugan is depicted being married to two divine consorts (Valli and Deviyani), in the Aryan (or Northern India) he is shown as an eternal bachelor. The reason for his celibacy holds interest in that it also involves his mother, Devi Parvati. Murugan as Skanda, an army general and also the son of Shiva was very handsome and a very masculine god. He was his mother's favorite, so this gave him a lot of leeway with all the other gods, goddesses, and other celestial beings. He was also a favorite among girls, and loved to play with and tease them on a regular basis.

When his mother heard about his teasing, she not only reprimanded him, but she also showed him her own image in every woman. This affected Karthikeyan so much that he took the vow of celibacy and remained forever a bachelor (or Kumara).

But there is a twist to this story (in the Dravidian culture) because here Lord Murugan is shown not only as married, but he also has two consorts. Not to worry, on a deeper level they are not 'wives' in the worldly sense. Valli and Deviyani only represent his will power and his power of action. They also

148

represent the two aspects of Murugan devotees whereas the vel of Murugan is used to pierce the ignorance of the devotee.

Murugan is also a mystical god. He represents Yoga and renunciation and his devotees undertake severe penance or vows like the 'Kavadi', rolling on the ground around his temple premises and even 'girivallam' which is walking around the mountains on which his temple is situated.

The story of Lord Murugan losing the 'jnana pazham' (fruit of knowledge) to his brother Ganesha is well known and mentioned previously. But this story also has another version. It is believed the contest was not for the fruit of knowledge but for marrying 'Riddhi' and 'Siddhi' the daughters of a King. But Lord Murugan had already taken the vow of celibacy and was committed to renunciation. So though he was a *jnani,* He knowingly lost the contest and pretended to be angry so he could give up his family. So he left Mount Kailasha where his parents and brother lived and came down to Palani to live as an ascetic.

Eventually Lord Ganesha, his elder brother was married to Riddhi and Siddhi.

Vetrivel Muruganukku Arohara

Glory to Bhagavan Ramana Maharshi for narrating this tale. In the story of Vetrivel Muruganukku Arohara legend tells us that a devotee once spoke to Murugan about an illness, the doctor's treatment of him, and the kind of services that servants rendered to him. No reply was given by Murugan. However, in the evening during the gathering of all devotees, Murugan took oil and started massaging his own legs. With a smile on his face, he answered the questioner with symbolism stating that each person is his own doctor as well as servant. What a beautiful teaching by Murugan himself!

The questioner then asked Murugan what is to be done if, unlike Murugan (still massaging his own legs), someone does not have enough strength to do the same. At this Murugan replied that if we have enough strength to eat different kinds of things and satiate the palate, then why shouldn't a person have adequate strength to massage himself and do his or her own things? Naturally, to this, the questioner was not able to find any answer at all, so he remained silent and bent his head to pay obeisance.

Murugan then began to narrate the following story. To be a Mutt's (Hindu religious congregation) head, a particular *sanyasi* became very anxious and toiled mentally and

150

physically. For this, some disciples were required and accordingly he tried to secure a few for himself. Disciples who came found that the *sanyasi* had limited knowledge and hence never enlisted. This led to a problem. Once the *sanyasi* had to visit the city but with no disciples there was no special attention received by his visit. To ensure that no one came to know about this, he decided to keep his clothes bundle hidden away. Because nobody observed the proper ritual for him on his arrival at a house, afterwards, he could pretend that he had reached there at an earlier time and his hosts would not know he had placed them there himself. Usually disciples were supposed to carry out chores for a master; this showed that the *sanyasi* was of good standing and a respected one.

The *sanyasi* later tried entering a house using his plan, but found there were people around most of the time. Finally he found a house with an open door and no one home. He entered the house and in a corner placed the bundle and sat in the verandah. When the owner enquired about him, he said that he was a Mutt's head and had arrived at the city on work. He said that he had come to that house because he knew that she was a good person and hence sent his belongings with a disciple to her home to stay the night there and move out the very next morning. She said that nobody had come with any bundle but he insisted that it was there. She called him in and served him food to eat. Later that night she queried about the disciple and commented that he had not come back yet. To this the *sanyasi* said that the useless disciple must have eaten food in the market and could be wandering. The lady asked the *sanyasi* to sleep and said that she would open the door for the disciple if he came. To make the couple of the house believe him the *sanyasi* continued to enact this drama that he had a disciple who had brought his luggage and bundle of clothes for two nights.

Since there really was no disciple, he pretended to open and close the door for the disciple, pretended to ask the disciple questions, and even shouted at the imaginary disciple to make it look real and to make his host believe him. The couple kept observing this pretense through a small hole in the wall. He also kept changing his voice tone to convince the couple that the disciple existed. The next morning the couple spied the *sanyasi* pretending to drive out the disciple and asked him to complete some jobs and only then return.

The couple hid the bundle when the *sanyasi* was bathing and when he returned told him that the disciple came and took it, saying that the *sanyasi* had asked him to bring the bundle to him. They also said that this was the same disciple he had shouted at and who had massaged the *sanyasi's* legs on a previous night. To this, the *sanyasi* had nothing to say and left the home. While narrating the story, Bhagavan Ramana states that when a disciple serves this is what is really happening. Every person should be his or her own servant. Bhagavan

Ramana then, with fists and hands, pretends to massage his own legs.

MURUGAN AND KUMARAGURUPARAR

SWAMIGAL

Kumaraguruparar Swamigal wrote the seventeenth century classic, the Kandar Kalivenba, in praise of Murugan of Tiruchendur. He was a Masilamanidesigar disciple of the fourth Dharmapuram Adheenam (mutt) head and the founder of Kashi Mutt, better known as Thiruppananthal Adheenam. He was born in the year 1625 A.D on Tambaraparani's northern bank and nineteen miles away from Tiruchendur, to a Saiva Vellala family.

His parents, Sivakami Ammaiyar and Sikhamani Kavirayar, underwent a long period of penance to please Murugan of Tiruchendur, after which Murugan blessed them with a child. Until the boy reached five years of age he was unable to speak. Seeing this, the parents felt deeply pained and again resorted to penance to gain a boon from Murugan of Tiruchendur. They were very anxious to hear their child speak. They waited for months together hoping for some signs of speech in their child but to no avail.

By that time, they had made a decision that if the child was dumb, they would throw themselves into the sea and then drown themselves. Still, no signs of speech were observed in the child. With this they made up their minds. Finally, taking the little one along, the parents went and waded deep into the sea, and kept walking towards the horizon up to their necks, and were about to drown. The water rose as if to test them and then suddenly a human form appeared with a flower in hand who spoke to the child asking him what this was all about.

To the parents surprise the child started speaking when being questioned by the holy form. He began praising Murugan with "Poomevusenggamalap..." words which actually are the poem Kandar Kalivenba's opening lines. This is a 244 line poem which praises the gods, and the Saiva Siddhanta truths. At the feet of Murugan then, the child and his father studied Tamil and attained the highest levels of proficiency, purely on account of divine grace. This was just the beginning of a life that was to lead others into prayer and worship.

Eventually he attained manhood and took to a life of austerity. Finally, he took the decision to leave home. All through the Tamil region he wandered and visited places that were renowned pilgrimage sites. It is said that he composed numerous poems about each of the deities to whom he paid obeisance. He found peace and closeness to his inner self and to god in his poems and songs. Kumaraguruparar moved from Tiruvarur to Dharmapuram even as his mind kept signaling to him something great that was supposed to unfold.

He kept satiating inner turmoil as he proceeded along the preordained path, without a clue of what was to happen next.

In the tradition of Saiva Siddhanta, the mutt or the Adheenam is housed and maintained by the town. Srila Sri Masilamani Desigar was responsible for decorating the mutt's presidency. Obeisance was paid by Kumaraguruparar to the saint on arrival at the mutt. Here Kumaraguruparar was asked by Desigar to explain the Periya Puranam song and highlight its significance. Now *this* was the kind of guru Kumaraguruparar was looking for! At the behest of the guru, he was not only graced and blessed but also granted initiation into a life of renouncement.

To pay respects to the guru, Kumaraguruparar went to Dharmapuram on four different occasions. In Tirupanandhal, Kumbakonam District, in Tamil Nadu he built the Kashi Mutt. His devotion was persistent and pure and in this he was bestowed the grace of being a truly exemplar devotee. He provided a lot of support to Hinduism in the region, spread Shaivism from 1658 to 1688 and for three decades he lived a blessed life at Kashi. His life was an example of simple living and lofty deeds. In May 1688, Kumaraguruparar attained *Samadhi*, at Kashi.

His quest for the guru, renunciation, and the path opened to him are indicative of the fact (stated in the Vedas) that a true seeker need not step out to find the guru, the guru will himself call for the devotee. The life of the saint and his devotion to Murugan is an example of the great things that unfold when the heart is pure.

AMRITA VALLI AND AIRAVATAM

Those not familiar with Hindu Mythology may find the idea of two wives for gods a strange idea. But the esoteric meaning in the symbolization of two wives has a deeper meaning that can only be revealed by a deeper study. The two wives of Murugan, Deviyani and Valli actually symbolize the two types of devotees who strive for union with the Supreme.

Murugan fought Surapadman and his army at various places but the six battle houses hold significance for every Murugan devotee. Thiruparankundram, the first battle house, is known as the 'Relationship and Attraction' house. Here Lord Murugan marries his divine consort Deviyani in the traditional and orthodox style of marriage. The temple continues to attract devotees even to this day who come here to pray and perform 'pooja' for cordial marital relationships.

Murugan married Deviyani in the traditional, orthodox way and she also represents devotees who follow the scriptures rigidly observing the injunctions. They are followers of Vaidika Karma, and sincerely believe in seeking Murugan by following rituals and rules. Valli on the other hand represents those devotees who are more emotional and believe more in the right mental attitude than in any rules or rituals. Murugan marries Valli in the Gandharva style of marriage. Murugan wooed Valli rather than the other way round. Devotees like Valli are so immersed in the love of Murugan that Murugan himself comes seeking them. He manifested both love and force while seeking Valli's hand, love for her while Murugan used force to eliminate her relatives. But again Valli's love won over because at her request Murugan restored life back to all her slain Veddan relatives.

But Deviyani and Valli also have another story. Lord Vishnu has two beautiful daughters called Amrita Valli and Sundara Valli. Having heard of the greatness of Shiva's son both fall in love with Lord Murugan when he stays at Kanda Verpu. Both express their desire to marry him, and perform severe penance at Sharavana Poigai where Murugan was born. Murugan, pleased with their devotion, ordained that they be born again and agreed to marry them both in their next birth.

Accordingly Sundara Valli was born as Valli to Siva Muni who impregnated a gazelle and was adopted by a hunter-chieftain called Nambirajan. Amritha Valli in the meantime took the form of a young female child and went to meet Lord Indra at Mount Meru. She told Indra she was the daughter of Vishnu and now the responsibility of looking after her became Indra's duty. Lord Indra was only too glad to look after Amritha Valli.

Like all celestial beings and gods, Lord Indra too has his own 'vahana' or vehicle. He rides a white elephant, Airavatam, who is also called by different names like 'Ardha—Matanga' or

159

elephant of the clouds. Airavatam is a spotless white elephant that has four tusks and seven trunks and he is also called Arkasodara, brother of the sun. When Amrita Valli came to Devaloka, Lord Indra entrusted her to the care of Airavatam.

Airavatam brought up the child with love and affection and she came to be known as Deviyani, or the one brought by the celestial elephant. After the *Surasamharam*, Indra and other devatas were grateful to Lord Murugan for destroying the demons. Lord Indra offered Deviyani's hand in marriage since she was by then of marriageable age to Lord Murugan. He was already aware of Deviyani's penance to marry him as Vishnu's daughter and readily agrees to the marriage.

The marriage of Deviyani and Murugan took place at Thiruparankundram with the blessings of both Murugan's parents, Shiva—Parvati, Lord Vishnu, Lord Brahma, Murugan's brother, Lord Ganesha, and all the celestial beings. After which everyone joyously returned to their own abode and started to continue with their duties and activities

The marriage (or union) was celebrated after the defeat of dark forces so it also symbolizes the destruction of vices before the union of *Jivatma* and *Paramatma* can take place. The story also illustrates the single-minded penance and devotion that Deviyani showed to attain her goal. She represents the ritualistic aspect of Murugan and his devotees.

Rahul Kabade

Since Deviyani was brought by an elephant, the story also illustrates that animals have souls too and they can love and care just like humans.

ALAGAMUTTU PULAVAR – MURUGAN'S

FORTUNATE DEVOTEE

Lord Murugan is worshipped by his devotees either by saying his main *mantra* Om Saravanabhava, reciting the Kanda shashti kavacham, or verses from Shanmukha Bhujamgam. The Kandar Alankaram provides enough material for the devotees to praise Murugan. There are, however, innumerable poets and sages who have been inspired by the beauty and wisdom of the merciful Murugan and have left beautiful works of devotion praising their favorite deity.

Murugan legends are as many as his names and forms, the best part of Murugan devotion being that each devotee can experience Him on a personal level in his own, unique way. But none have been as fortunate as Alagamuttu Pulavar whose story was narrated by Swami Sivananda. Alagamuttu lived about 200 years ago. His story is similar to another great poet, Kalidasa; only Pulavar was blessed by Murugan and not Saraswati as was the case with Kalidasa.

Alagamuttu, who was a simple accountant at the Nagai Subrahmanya temple, was blessed by Lord Murugan in person and went on to become one of the finest poets of his time. Alagamuttu was a pious man and an ardent devotee of Lord Murugan with the habit of eating just the 'prasadam' from the temple at night. It is believed that one night after a hard day's toil Alagamuttu fell soundly asleep inside the temple. The temple priests tried calling him and receiving no answer, locked the temple and went home.

Alagamuttu, unaware of these events, woke up in the middle of the night only to find he was alone and locked inside the temple. To his utter dismay he also felt extremely hungry and thirsty. Since there was nobody to help him, he started praying to Murugan to quench his thirst and hunger. Lord Murugan then assumed the form of an old priest and appeared in front of Alagamuttu and asked him what he wanted. Since he was so hungry he asked for food and water and Murugan presented him with a feast. Once Alagamuttu had his fill, his 'puravakarmas' (past karmas) were also washed away as he ate the divine food and he stood before Murugan himself in his pristine form.

The priest then requested Alagamuttu to sing a few songs to praise Murugan, but Alagamuttu, a simple accountant, was astonished at such a request and expressed his helplessness. Lord Murugan then showed his true form with six faces, twelve arms and his various weapons in full splendor. He ordained that Alagamuttu shall sing songs with his divine grace. It was no dream either, because Alagamuttu was completely awake and he was flooded with the divine light emanating from Murugan's form.

The next day when the priests came back to open the temple they were shocked to find Alagamuttu inside the temple singing ecstatic songs to Murugan. From then on Alagamuttu Pulavar came to be known as a great poet and saint. He lived at the temple singing divine inspirational songs in praise of his favorite deity.

The end of Pulavar is as fascinating as his entire life. This most fortunate devotee of Lord Murugan went on a long pilgrimage and stayed at a place called Shiyali. He meditated here on Murugan and gave up his mortal body. At the same time, in his favorite temple of Murugan in Nagai, the priests saw him rushing into the temple in a great hurry. Since he was held in awe and respected by them, nobody stopped or questioned Alagamuttu. They simply expected him to come out of the shrine. But Alagamuttu did not come out. He simply became 'one' with his dearest Murugan.

This concept of 'here and there' as demonstrated by Alagamuttu's body and soul is a fine example of Murugan's manifestation of 'ippo—enge' (here and now). Just as he is omnipresent, his devotees can reach that divine stage too with his blessings.

Pulavar's story is also a great example of the things that can be achieved in both the material and spiritual path with single-minded devotion and simple thoughts and actions. Murugan also works in mysterious ways to bestow his grace on different devotees. Nobody can be sure when or what type of boon he will grant. But there is no doubt that he is always present to hear the prayers of devotees.

NAKKIRAR POEMS ON MURUGAN

During the Sangam period in a Pandiyan Kingdom, poet Nakkirar was very famous. He was, in fact, the court poet. He was well versed with the Tamil language. Once, however, he was imprisoned by a demon. This is a story of Lord Murugan saving Poet Nakkirar from the demon.

Once, a Pandiyan King had a doubt. He wanted to know if the scent that comes from female hair is natural or artificial. He asked all of the court poets of the Pandiyan Kingdom. Everyone told him their opinion. But the king wasn't satisfied with their answers.

So the Pandiyan King asked Poet Nakkirar. Nakkirar told him that the scent which comes from women's hair is artificial, and though the Pandiyan king was expecting a more detailed answer than this, Poet Nakkirar couldn't give it to him. So the Pandiyan King decided to ask all the poets in the entire Kingdom. He announced that the perfect answer would win one thousand gold coins.

Knowing this, Lord Shiva decided to play a game with Poet Nakkirar regarding his knowledge of Tamil literacy, and to do so he sent Poet Tharmi to answer the King's question. Lord Shiva composed a poem for Poet Tharmi, thus giving him the perfect answer to read out to the Pandiyan King. Later, Poet

Rahul Kabade

Tharmi read the poem for King Pandiyan and this satisfied the king very much. Accordingly, the king awarded Poet Tharmi with the promised one-thousand gold coins.

At that time Poet Nakkirar raised a question. He asked Poet Tharmi to explain the poem. Since Tharmi didn't write it, he couldn't explain the poem. Poet Nakkirar also pointed out that there was a fault in the poem, and told the King that he shouldn't award Tharmi with gold coins. So Poet Tharmi was made to go empty handed. When Lord Shiva came to know about the incident, He was of course angry with Poet Nakkirar for judging the poem was wrong. Lord Shiva immediately went to the king's court as a poet and pointed out that the poem was correct, but still, Poet Nakkirar refused to accept it. Furious, Lord Shiva showed his true form and asked if the poem was still wrong.

Poet Nakkirar now realized that it was Lord Shiva who came as a poet, but still he told him that the poem has faults. Lord Shiva was amazed by the spirit of Nakkirar. He was also amazed to see that Poet Nakkirar was confident with his answer. Lord Shiva blessed Poet Nakkirar, but at the same time Nakkirar realized that it was his grave fault to speak against Lord Shiva this way. He apologized and Lord Shiva asked him to go on a pilgrimage.

Nakkirar went to many temples. On the way, he was imprisoned by a giant demon. This demon used to capture a

167

hundred humans each day and eat them only when he reached a count of one hundred. On this particular day, Nakkirar was the hundredth person to be caught and he realized that the giant was going to eat everyone. At the same time, the other ninety-nine people already in captivity blamed Poet Nakkirar. They told him it was because of him that they were all going to be eaten, he being the hundredth. Nakkirar was very sad. He didn't want the giant demon to eat any of them.

From his prison Poet Nakkirar worshiped Lord Murugan. He asked Lord Murugan to save them all and he composed a special poem just for Lord Murugan to release them. The poem is called Tirumurugarruppatai. He was sincere with his prayers. Lord Murugan was pleased with Poet Nakkirar's prayers and made his presence known in front of the demon, thus killing and destroying the demon. Then he released all hundred people including Poet Nakkirar, blessing him. Poet Nakkirar continued his pilgrimage thanking Lord Murugan all the way. Today, reciting Tirumurugarruppatai will always help us when we are in need or in danger. It has the power to deliver us from harm.

When Nakkirar was imprisoned he not only prayed for his freedom, but also prayed for the ninety-nine others in captivity. Through this story Murugan teaches us to care and pray for everyone around us.

MUTTUSWAMI DEEKSHITAR

Lord Murugan is sometimes known as the god of antiquity because of his presence during the various Yugas. But his miracles have not ceased as Kali Yuga Vardhan. He has been granting boons to scores of his devotees, and some of the most famous ones in Kali Yuga are Arunagirinathar, Thiru Jnana Sambandhar, Sri Ramana Maharishi and Sri Muttuswami Deekshitar.

Sri Muttuswami Deekshitar (March 24, 1775 to October 21, 1835) is the youngest amongst the musical trinity of Carnatic music composers. Sri Thyagaraja and Sri Syama Sastri are the other two of the trinity. They mostly composed in Telugu while Deekshitar is known for his Sanskrit compositions.

According to Subbaram Deekshitar, a childless couple, Ramaswamy Deekshitar and his wife, visited the Vaidhyeshwaran Kovil (temple) which is now situated 140 miles from present day Chennai. They prayed to Vaidyanaatha and his divine consort Balambaal for a child and performed pooja and austerities for forty-five days, or one mandalam. The goddess then appeared in their dream and presented them with a pearl necklace and it is also the reason why his parents called him Muttuswami when a boy was born to them. 'Muthu' (muttu) means pearl.

The boy was born in Tiruvarur and his father, who himself was a composer, met a Naatha Yogi when he visited Chidambaram. On the Yogi's request Muttuswami went to Kashi with the Yogi, who trained him in Shakti upasana. Later, when the yogi felt Muttuswami's training was over, he asked him to stand on the banks of the river Ganga and wish for any boon. A silver veena musical instrument appeared out of the river and Deekshitar mastered the veena and is always depicted holding it in his hands. After the Yogi attained *Samadhi*, Muttuswami returned to his hometown. But his guru had also instructed him to visit the Lord Murugan temple at Tiruttani.

Accordingly Muttuswami went to the temple and was immersed in deep meditation sitting on the steps of the temple. An old man appeared in front of Deekshitar and asked him to open his mouth and placed a sugar candy on his tongue and disappeared immediately. When Deekshitar opened his mouth again he had a vision of Murugan in all his glory. Deekshitar burst out his first composition 'Shri Nathadi Guruguho Jayathi Jayathi' (which when translated means 'Let Sri Natha Yogi and Lord Guru Guha win'). Later the 'GuruGuha' became his signature for all his works.

Lord Murugan works in mysterious ways and though sometimes he Himself appears to his devotees, sometimes he works *through* his devotees to bring about a miracle. When Deekshitar visited the temple of Thiruparankundram, the temple artist Thambiappan who played a special drum called 'shuddha maddalam' suffered a severe stomach ache. Since allopathic treatment was unheard of in those days, the pundits suggested reciting the Navagraha Sooktham for relief, a part of Krishna Yajur Veda. But Thambiappan was a non-Brahmin, so according to the practice at that time, he could not chant the Vedas, since they were chanted only by Brahmins.

Deekshitar then composed the 'Navagraha Kritis', which a non-Brahmin *could* chant, and needless to say, Thambiappan was cured of his illness after Deekshitar taught him. The songs reflect a profound knowledge of the *mantra* to cure illness and using astrology (jyotisha shastra).

Deekshitar also visited the Tiruchendur temple and composed 300 songs that are still sung today during *Surasamharam* which is enacted every year at Tiruchendur.

There were many more miraculous incidents in the life of Muttuswami Deekshitar. Once Deekshitar went to a temple dedicated to Lord Shiva namely, Akshaya Linga Swami temple at Kivalur. Since it was noon, the temple priest was closing the doors. Even after repeated requests from Deekshitar the priest refused to open the temple doors. But, undeterred, Deekshitar started singing the 'Akshayalina vibho' kriti and the door of the sanctum sanctorum opened of its own accord and Deekshitar had a darshan of his deity.

Deekshitar left his mortal coil on the eve of a Dipawali while his students sat around him singing songs composed by him in praise of goddess Lakshmi.

All the incidents in and around the life of, Deekshitar show that Murugan works in the most mysterious ways and truly, some of his leelas will never be understood by everyone.

Rahul Kabade

THE STORY OF CHELLAPPA SWAMI

Amongst the many saints and sages of Sri Lanka, Chellappa Swami is the strangest of all. He lived most of his life like a mad man in his outward appearance. But he initiated many great yogis into Murugan worship, one of whom was Yoga Swami.

Chellappa Swami (1840—1914) was the son of a farmer and the family lived on the eastern side of the Nallur Murugan temple. Chellappa studied in the Central College and later worked in the Kacheri (Legal premises/office). But from a young age Chellappa never showed much interest in worldly affairs and was always drawn towards Kumaran, a form of Murugan and the presiding deity at Nallur.

Chellappa Swami himself was initiated into the siddha line of yoga by another yogi called Kadai Swami (1810—1875) who came to Sri Lanka from India. After his *Jiva Samadhi* at Neeravaidai, Chellappa Swami continued the line of spiritual gurus at Nallur temple.

Chellappa Swami enjoyed a very intense relationship with Kumaran of Nallur and was a liberated soul. He sat by the theradi, the path of the chariot, at the temple uttering 'vakyas', or great utterances. Since he appeared to be slightly mad he never wrote any books. But his disciples compiled his great utterances that offered insight into the soul of a true devotee. He believed in 'everything is right', we (humans) know nothing', 'Truth, truth everywhere' and 'It has been accomplished long ago'.

His disciple Yoga Swami continues to guide other devotees in the line of Kumaran worship and Chellappa's *Samadhi* which is the center of the temple continues to draw devotees to this day. They also sing his praises and recite some of his sayings with devotion.

A true devotee of Lord Murugan, Chellappa Swami was turned into a saint by the grace of Murugan and ended up teaching the younger generation about religion. Knowledge cannot be destroyed and its power attracts and affects all.

Chellappa's life proves that there is no need to know the Vedas, or any holy scriptures to find Murugan. He lives in the heart of the devotees as Guha and will manifest in any form he likes. There is no need to follow rituals or strict austerities to realise the presence of Murugan. True devotion, no matter how simple it is, will always bring Murugan's blessings.

THE EIGHTEEN SIDDHA'S

The very word 'siddha' means a person who has realized the non-duality of the *Jivatma*. Such a siddha has realized that the *atman* and *Paramatma* are one and the same. A siddha can also mean someone who has attained perfection in all levels of physical, mental, intellectual, vital and spiritual being. According to the different ancient works available to date, there are eighteen prominent siddhas. Though later several siddhas came into being, these particular eighteen masters have a prominent place at the Palani temple of Dandayudhapani.

The first siddha is Agastya, and the rest are Thirumoolar, Bhogar, Machamuni, Karuvurar, Ramadevar, Konkanar, Nandidevar, Valmiki, Sundaranadar, Korakkar, Dhanvanthri, Idaikkadar, Kamalamuni, Sattaimuni, Pambattisiddhar, Patanjali and Kuthambi Siddha.

Though each of them knew every aspect of Yoga, medicine and alchemy, each left a work that was unique to them. Sage Agastya was the first disciple of Shiva and after meditating in Mount Kailasha and learning from the Aadi Guru Shiva, he travelled to the South. Agastya, who only knew Sanskrit, was taught the Tamil language by none other than Murugan. He is also known to have brought about the fusion of the two cultures—Aryan and Dravidian (Northern and Southern India).

175

His disciples are Babaji, Bhogar, Thiruvalluvar and Machamuni. His work on Tamil Grammar is the greatest ancient work of Tamil literature. He also contributed in making kayakalpa, Yoga and medicine. He attained *Samadhi* at Ananthashayana but people believe he still lives on, in the astral plane.

Nandidevar is another direct disciple of Lord Shiva and his contribution includes works on natural sciences, alchemy, philosophy, yoga and kaykalpa. His disciples are Sattaimuni, Patanjali, Thirumoolar, Dakshinamurthy and Romarishi. His *Jiva Samadhi* is located at Kashi.

Thirumoolar was the disciple of Nandidevar and his contribution includes Yoga and philosophy. His work 'Thirumandiram' (God-Mantra) is still available and his *Samadhi* is at Thiruvavaduthurai 10 miles near Kumbhakonam temple.

Bhogar is further famous disciple of Agastya but he also studied under another Sage Kalangi Nathar and is considered to be the greatest alchemist of all time because of his 'nava pashanam' idol of Lord Murugan at Palani. To this day nobody has been able to work out the composition of the idol. His disciples include, Babaji, Konkanavar, Karuvoorar, Pulipani and Idaikadar. His *Jiva Samadhi* is at the Palani temple though again he is available to disciples even today.

Bhogar's disciple Konkanavar is known for his works on yoga, philosophy and religion of which there are, in total, twenty five works that are available. He has over 557 disciples and his *Jiva Samadhi* is at Tirupati.

Machamuni trained under Agastya, Pasundar and Punnakeesar and is also known as Matsyendranath. There are ten known works on Hatha yoga and tantric practices. His *Samadhi* is at Thiruparankundram and his eminent disciple is Gorakanathar.

Gorakanathar was initiated by three gurus Dattatreya (another aspect of Vishnu), Allama Prabhu and Machamuni. His works includes the "Avadhuta Gita' and thirteen other works on Hatha yoga, order of ascetics and his *Samadhi* is at Poyur.

Sattaimuni was initiated by Dakshinamurthy and Nandidevar. His works of alchemy, yoga and medicine are still available and he attained *Samadhi* at Srirangam. His prominent disciples were Paambatti siddhar and Sundaranadar.

Sundaranadar trained under both Sattaimuni and Konkanavar and his twenty four known works on medicine and philosophy are still available, while he attained *Samadhi* at Kudal (Madurai).

Ramadevar was the disciple of Pulastiyar and Karuvoorar and is also known as 'mandira siddha' because of his extensive knowledge in magic. He attained *Samadhi* at Alagar Malai and his works include *mantra shastra* and another twenty-four works.

Kuthambi siddhar was initiated by Alukkani siddhar and his *Samadhi* is at Mayavaram.

Karuvurar was another disciple of Bhogar and his contribution includes the construction of the 10,000—year old Tanjore temple. His *Samadhi* is at Karuvai (Karur). Idaikadar was his disciple.

Idaikadar trained under both Karuvurar and Bhogar. His contribution includes texts on kayakalpa and his *Samadhi* is at Tiruvannamalai.

Kamalamuni contributed in medicine and philosophy and two known works of his are still available today and his *Samadhi* is at Aarur (Tiruvaram).

Valmiki was initiated by Sage Narada and his best work is the Ramayana and his *Samadhi* is at Ettikudi.

Dhanvanthri contributed in the fields of medicine and kayakalpa; twenty-two known works of his are still available. His *Samadhi* is at Vaideeswaran Kovil in Chennai.

Patanjali is also known as the father of yoga and he was initiated by Nandidevar. His *Samadhi* is at Rameshwaram.

Paambatti siddhar was initiated by Sattaimuni and he was a snake charmer before becoming a siddha. His *Samadhi* is at Harishankaran Kovil.

When visiting the Palani temple, one cannot miss the statues of these eighteen great siddha's who have given humanity its wealth of spiritual knowledge and wisdom. They continue to inspire their followers and guide their lineages even to this day.

MURUGAN IN TRIBAL TRADITIONS

Murugan has been worshipped over the ages by different sects of people. His marriage to both Devasena and Valli is seen as an attempt to unite all Hindus irrespective of whether they are Saivaites or Vaisanavas.

Murugan has an effect on the geographical, cultural, social, cosmological as well as metaphysical levels in India and, in fact, wherever he is worshipped predominantly. Geographically Murugan pervades over the south of India and south Asia including Sri Lanka, Malaysia, Singapore and the Fiji islands.

Culturally since he is known as the 'Tamizh Kaduval', the life of Murugan has a direct impact on the Tamil culture and its claim of divine origin. On the social level because Murugan is depicted as married to two spouses at the same time and because of their acceptance, the concept of 'co-wife' has also achieved some acceptance in Tamil culture. Murugan also led the celestial army in the war against the demons and therefore, on the cosmological level, he represents the constant war of good over evil. But the most important aspect of Murugan is on the metaphysical level because he is known to have taught the meaning of the sacred 'Om' to both Brahma and Lord Shiva.

But apart from all this, Murugan also holds a very interesting place in the tribal traditions. The meanings of the leelas of Murugan in the Skanda Purana are too complicated to be understood on a simple level. So interpreting different stories to understand their meaning and relevance becomes easy when it is done through song and dance, so the metaphysical takes a very physical form.

Sangam Kaalam is also known as the golden period of Tamil literature because it produced some of the greatest works in Tamil. But at the same time the Kurava people living in the mountains had their own traditions, especially about their 'Kula swami' Murugan.

The Kuravas believed that their virgin girls were troubled by the touch of Murugan so in order to get rid of it they celebrated 'Veriyattu'. It is a celebration that is done at midnight inside the open space of a house. The place is decorated beautifully with Sevvari and other fragrant flowers and manal (a decorative sand). Murugan is then invited with different types of food and musical instruments. The Murugan flag with the rooster symbol is hoisted while offering flowers and a paste made from ghee and white gingili. He is invited to sit on his 'Kadambu' seat and his vehicle the peacock and his weapon the 'vel' are also praised in songs sung by those gathered.

A goat that is sliced is also hung on a tree and its blood mixed with millet is offered as 'Bali' (sacrifice offering) to Murugan.

181

As the dances commence, with many different musical instruments playing, it is believed Murugan himself comes down and dances with the Kurava girls, holding their hands. He is described as the 'Velan' or one holding the spear in this context of tribal celebrations. He drinks toddy and enjoys dancing with the girls on the boulders. This almost human aspect of Murugan in the tribal traditions shows that he is never far from his devotees. There is no need for specific *mantras* or rituals to seek his blessings. We can pray to him in any form and he manifests to suit the need and situation.

As the tribes pray for rain and fertility, Murugan, in his benevolence, blesses them with a life that is free of disease, hunger and enmity. Though later the tribal dances and their celebration were recorded in works like 'Anankutai Murugan', this celebration of dance and music in praise of Murugan also shows those traditions that have no written texts can be carried down through the ages by word-of-mouth and traditional beliefs live on. Murugan as the Kuranji Kaduval (god of mountains) lives on in present day in remote tribal areas and 'Velan' continues to dance, play, and bless his devotees.

Rahul Kabade

MURUGAN AS KARTHIKEYA — THE FERTILITY

GOD OF BENGAL

The *avatar* of Karthikeya bears great significance in the path to enlightenment of the soul because he is the manifestation of the inner-grace needed to ascend the eternal path of life. The Skanda *avatar* of Murugan demonstrates the constant struggle between ignorance and wisdom. The Skanda Purana also teaches the importance of guru in life's journey.

Karthikeyan is also an individual of perfection; he is viewed as incredibly brutal and the most masculine among the gods. In his Kumara aspect he is handsome and represents eternal youth. Karthikeya, as the god of war and victory, guided the celestial beings to victory over the demons. As 'Senthil' he is also known as the formidable one. The reason for his different forms is always to bless his devotees in various situations that need divine guidance.

Since the metaphysical aspect of worshipping god needs single-mindedness and rigorous practices, various methods were devised to bring a union between the metaphysical and physical world. One aspect of which is to carve idols that represent various gods and then to worship them. The other is to write down stories of their legends, valor, mercy, and virtuous deeds that can be passed on to generations.

183

The Vedas, Upanishads, the Bhagavad Gita, and the Puranas were written for the betterment of humanity and the continuation of divine guidance for eternity. However the Puranas in their pure form cannot be understood by common people, so stories and legends were interwoven to make it easy for everyone. Though the ultimate goal of any Purana is to direct a person in their day-to-day life and struggles towards God, they also taught that the journey was full of joy and pain. These two came as a package and had to be accepted with equanimity by the seeker. The Puranas and, in particular Skanda Purana, help a devotee in everyday existence when faced with such decision.

Devotees who pray for material achievements also have their prayers answered though Murugan in his infinite mercy which will also pave the way for spiritual growth. So prayers for things like good education, good health, a good marriage and the birth of children can be conducted with faith and Murugan answers them without exception.

From time immemorial a male child was considered the carrier of a family line and devotees always prayed to Karthikeya for this boon. Even in the great epic Rig-Veda Naigamesa, or Nejamesa, an aspect of Muruga was known as the guardian and protector of children. He was also known as the deity who granted the boon of children to childless couples. To this day

Murugan (as Karthikeya) is worshiped by women who desire a male child.

As cultures and traditions evolved over a period of time, different places, in similar fashion, have their own legends. Karthikeya has even been linked to the Indus valley civilization. Historically, too, there are many mentions of Karthikeya, and as was mentioned earlier, the Gupta age had two Kings named after him—Kumaragupta and Skandagupta.

In Tamil Nadu and other parts of the south, Murugan is worshipped as the god of wisdom, justice, divine mercy from Sangam Kaalam. In West Bengal, Murugan is considered to be the fertility god. During Durga puja he is worshipped along with Parvati (his mother and another aspect of Durga), for the birth of a male child in the family.

In West Bengal there is a tradition of hiding a small idol or image of Karthikeya on the premises of newly-married couples. This is done in the hope that the couple will be blessed with a male child.

The most important part of Murugan worship is that just reciting his '*moola mantra*', Om Sharavana Bhava, is enough to get his blessings. In Bengal, though Karthikeya is part of the elaborate Durga Puja celebrations even shaping the cultural aspect of the place, seeking Murugan blessings on a personal level is as simple as just saying the moola *mantra* with devotion a few times.

Rahul Kabade

BHAGAVAN RAMANA MAHARISHI AND MURUGAN

Sri Bhagavan Ramana Maharishi (January 9, 1879 – April 14, 1950) was born into a traditional *Brahmin* family but he considered himself an *'Atiasram'* (or someone who has no attachments and caste restrictions). Though he did not believe in any doctrine, ritual or rules he had complete knowledge of all the sacred texts. He often quoted from 'Kandar Anbuthi' and 'Kandar Alangaram' (the divine hymns praising Lord Murugan written by another Kali Yuga Murugan devotee, Arunagirinathar).

Bhagavan Ramana Maharishi also personified the *'yogi'* and renunciation aspect of Lord Murugan to such a great extent that some of Maharishi's devotees believed he was an *avatar* of Murugan. But Maharishi himself did not believe in *avatars* or reincarnation. His one principle that was predominant in his teachings was 'the art of silence'.

Maharishi, though, did not have any formal education in spirituality or the scriptures. He had a normal education of that time because he studied in British schools—first in Scott's Middle School and then in American Mission High school. Even in his later life, after his self-realization, he spent most of his time in meditation and 'Mauna' (silence). But still, whenever asked a question, Maharishi could quote from the Puranas, Vedas, Upanishads and most of Aadi

187

Shankaracharya's works. He never left the abode of Arunachala mountain till the day of his *Maha Samadhi*.

The word Subrahmanya means someone who has knowledge of the 'Brahman' and that is the reason why Lord Murugan in his various forms is also known as 'Jnana Pundita' or the exponent of Supreme Knowledge. It is also said that it is Murugan who has authored the laws of Karma. The highest truth of any *'Jivatma'* is oneness with the Brahman and realization of this truth is called 'jnana' or true knowledge and this can only be attained after the 'third eye' of wisdom is opened. Murugan, who was born from the third eye of Shiva, embodies this state of the *atman*, and Maharishi also reached this state in his lifetime—this was the reason why most of his devotees believed him to be an *avatar* of Lord Murugan.

Maharishi spent his whole life in deep meditation at the Arunachala mountain in Tiruvannamalai, the mountain-abode of Lord Shiva in Southern India. Though Maharishi did not write any songs or hymns dedicated to Lord Murugan, his cryptic poems, just like Murugan, always try to reveal the workings of the inner planes of human existence.

Maharishi was not just a spiritual guru, he also was a poet with great vision and exemplary wisdom and his teachings were always about 'the quest'. He never gave direct answers and always asked the questioner more questions, which finally led to the questioner himself finding the answer.

His books reflect the way Maharishi lived because he never spoke much. He writes about the joys of complimenting Murugan or a chance for physical contact with an insect. He even writes about Lakshmi the cow and the mourning of her death.

Though Maharishi did not believe in miracles or initiating people into renunciation, miracles happened every day in his ashram and people gave up their worldly lives of luxury to stay back and serve Maharishi. Animals in and around the village surrounding the ashram were treated with kindness and people brought them to Maharishi when they were sick. He cared and looked after them till they got better.

Though Maharishi did not belong to the material world he understood the hardships of everyday living. People had tremendous faith in the nine planets or 'grahas' that affect human life. So he sung a hymn called 'Kolaru Pathikam' written by Thirugnanasambandhar which, when recited, removes the malefic effects of the planets.

Maharishi treated all humans and animals as equals. He ate very little food but whenever he ate food in the ashram it was shared amongst the rest of the devotees. Whenever people serving the food showed any partiality towards him, he stopped eating.

Lord Murugan, who works on the inner light of the human soul, always shows the path directly though sometimes he uses great personalities like Maharishi to show us the path. It becomes easy for people to understand the oneness of man and God through the life of masters such as Bhagavan Ramana Maharishi.

Rahul Kabade

SRI SUBRAHMANYA ASHTOTTARA

No offering to Murugan can be complete without reciting his
wonderful names and praising his glory and deeds by chanting
the Subrahmanya Ashtottara. While variations of this
Ashtottara are also available, this is the most popular one that
I have encountered so far.

!!Om Gam Ganapathaye Namaha!!

Om Skandaya Karthikeyaya Parvati Nandanayacha,
Mahadeva Kumaraya, Subrahmanyaya Tay Namaha.
!! Om Sharavana Bhava !!

Om Skandaya namaha
Om Guhaya namaha
Om Shanmukhaya namaha
Om Phalanetrasutaya namaha
Om Prabhave namaha
Om Pingalaya namaha
Om Krittikasunave namaha
Om Shikivahanaya namaha
Om Dvishadbhujaya namaha
Om Dvishannetraya namaha
Om Shaktidharaya namaha
Om Pishitasaprabhamjanaya namaha
Om Tarakasurasamharine namaha
Om Rakshobalavimardhanaya namaha
Om Mattaya namaha
Om Pramattaya namaha
Om Unmattaya namaha
Om Surasainyasurakshakaya namaha
Om Devasenapataye namaha

191

Om Prajnaya namaha
Om Kripalave namaha
Om Bhaktavatsalaya namaha
Om Umasutaya namaha
Om Shaktidharaya namaha
Om Kumaraya namaha
Om Kraunchadharanaya namaha
Om Senanyai namaha
Om Agnijanmane namaha
Om Vishakhaya namaha
Om Shankaratmajaya namaha
Om Shivasvamine namaha
Om Svaminathaya namaha
Om Sarvasvamine namaha
Om Sanatanaya namaha
Om Anantashaktaye namaha
Om Akshobhyaya namaha
Om Parvatipriyanandanaya namaha
Om Gangasutaya namaha
Om Sarodbhutaya namaha
Om Pavakatmajaya namaha
Om Ganasvamine namaha
Om Atmabhuve namaha
Om Jrumbhaya namaha
Om Prajrumbhaya namaha
Om Ujjrumbhaya namaha
Om Kamalasanasamstutaya namaha
Om Ekavarnaya namaha
Om Dvivarnaya namaha
Om Trivarnaya namaha
Om Sumanoharaya namaha
Om Chaturvarnaya namaha
Om Panchavarnaya namaha
Om Prajapataye namaha
Om Aharpataye namaha
Om Agnigarbhaya namaha
Om Samigarbhaya namaha
Om Vishvaretase namaha

Rahul Kabade

Om Surarighnaya namaha
Om Harodvarnaya namaha
Om Shubhakaranaya namaha
Om Vasavaya namaha
Om Vatuvesabhrte namaha
Om Pusne namaha
Om Gabhastine namaha
Om Gahanaya namaha
Om Chandravarnaya namaha
Om Kaladharaya namaha
Om Mayadharaya namaha
Om Mahamayine namaha
Om Kaivalyaya namaha
Om Sakalatmakaya namaha
Om Vishvayonaye namaha
Om Ameyatmane namaha
Om Tejonidhaye namaha
Om Anamayaya namaha
Om Paramesthine namaha
Om Parabrahmane namaha
Om Vedagharbaya namaha
Om Viradvapuse namaha
Om Pulindakanyabharte namaha
Om Mahasarasvatavrtaya namaha
Om Asritakhiladatre namaha
Om Choraghnaya namaha
Om Roganasanaya namaha
Om Anantamurtaye namaha
Om Anandaya namaha
Om Shikhandikritaketanaya namaha
Om Dhambhaya namaha
Om Paramadhambhaya namaha
Om Mahadhambaya namaha
Om Vrishakapaye namaha
Om Karanopattadehaya namaha
Om Karanatitavigrahaya namaha
Om Anishvaraya namaha
Om Amrutaya namaha
Om Pranaya namaha

Om Pranayamaparayanaya namaha
Om Vruddhahantre namaha
Om Viraghnaya namaha
Om Raktashyamagalaya namaha
Om Mahate namaha
Om Subrahmanyaya namaha
Om Guhaya namaha
Om Brahmanyaya namaha
Om Vanshavriddhikaraya namaha
Om Brahmanapriyaya namaha
Om Akshayaphalapradaya namaha
Om Vedavedhyaya namaha
Om Mayuravahanaye namaha
Om Sharavana Bhava

Iti Shree Subrahmanya Ashtottara Shatanaamavali Samaptam.